Will You Torment

a Windblown Leaf?

A Commentary on Job

Bill Cotton

Christian Focus Publications

Will you Torment a wind-blown Leaf?

Puzzled? The question is addressed by Job to God (13:25), and seems to sum up the essence of this incredible book. Job feels himself to be an unimportant nobody, a wind-blown leaf. Why should God waste his time tormenting such a being? Precisely because this NOBODY is a SOMEBODY to God, a person of immense importance.

© William Cotton
ISBN 185792 515 7
Published in 2001 by
Christian Focus Publications,
Geanies House, Fearn, Ross-shire,
IV20 1TW, Great Britian

The Bible Version used in this commentary is the New International Version, unless otherwise stated.

Cover design by Owen Daily

Printed and bound in Great Britain by
The Guernsey Press Co. Ltd., Guernsey, Channel Islands

Preface

I believe that you are going to enjoy this book by my friend and erstwhile colleague on Moorlands' staff, Bill Cotton. Here are some reasons why.

Firstly, it is the fruit of many years of close engagement with and teaching experience of that part of Scripture where many Christians struggle – the Old Testament. More specifically, as someone who has read Job often, and has preached from and lectured on it, I can testify that it is not an easy book. I know it is possible to get hold of the wrong end of the stick very quickly! This is where Bill proves to be a sure footed guide to this wonderful yet complex book.

Secondly, Bill helps us to feel Job's emotional turmoil and witness his personal *angst*. Wisely, he does not seek to silence the jarring notes or sandpaper away the rough edges of Job's unfolding drama too prematurely. Rather, we are led, step by painful step, to the ultimate answer to life's hard questions – the Mediator-Redeemer God!

If you are looking for a quick, slick answer to the problem of suffering – forget this commentary (and Job, for that matter!). But if you are prepared to invest a little time – and here the information boxes alone are worth the price of the book – then you will be rewarded with something far better than superficial answers: a deeper knowledge of the ways of God in Christ.

Dr Steve Brady
Principal
Moorlands College
Sopley,
Christchurch

Contents

Boxes

Introduction to Job

The book of Job is a remarkable book. Its message is not easy to grasp. A medical student told me recently that he had got through to chapter 10 and given it up! I understand his difficulty, and for that reason I have included a number of boxes scattered through the text. Read these first, and they will guide you through the main thrust of the various chapters. I have not the slightest doubt that reading his book will hold many rewards for the persistent reader of Job.

Chapters 1–2 tell the story of a rich and powerful, but thoroughly good man, called Job, who is suddenly stripped of his possessions, his family, his high place in society. His body is covered with the most awful sores, so that he is driven out of his town and reduced to living on a rubbish dump.

Chapters 3–27 give details of a lengthy argument between Job and three friends, whose initial objective was to bring comfort to this tormented man, but who end up ramming down his throat that he is a bad man who justifiably suffers for his evil. Job is just as certain that this is not so, and defends his corner stubbornly.

Chapter 28 is an interlude, a song in praise of wisdom.

Chapters 29–31 show Job presenting his final defence, asking God to show to him, to prove to the world, any wrong of which he might be guilty, and which merited his apparent punishment.

Chapters 32–37 recount the unexpected intervention of a young man, Elihu, who has been listening to the debate, and now proposes to give his own explanation.

In chapters 38–41, finally we hear the Lord speak to Job, and the mystery begins to unravel. Job humbles himself.

Chapter 42 declares Job totally restored, whilst his three friends are ordered to repent and ask Job to offer sacrifices for their sins.

OUTLINE OF JOB

The poet Tennyson is reputed to have called this book, "The greatest poem of ancient or modern times." It's a poetic masterpiece, one of the most original poems in the history of mankind, an artistic, created work, probably a poetic transformation of an original prose story.

I say a poetic transformation of a prose story because men do not sit on the ground and talk high poetry for hours on end, as Job and his friends do. Does this mean that the man Job never did exist in real life? Opinions vary. As early as the third century A.D., the Jewish Talmud affirmed,"Job did not exist and was not created; he is a parable." But Claus Westermann, a modern scholar, states: "What the narrative framework means is that the author is not speaking of an imaginary person but of Job, a real living human being, with a name and a particular domicile, just as his three friends are real men with names, living in this particular place."

T.H. Robinson also affirmed: "The poet (chs. 3-31) speaks out of the bitterness of his soul. We feel that the spiritual struggles which he records, perhaps even the physical sufferings he describes, can be nothing but his own experience. There is a poignancy of anguish, most of all spiritual anguish, which is wholly absent from the prose framework. The poem is inscribed with the heart's blood of the writer; the man who speaks there could not have taken the purely objective attitude of the narrator."

So we shall treat Job as a real man, not as a merely literary creation. Yet it may have been written some time after the events it describes, and is set in a poetic mould.

What is its theme, the author's intention?
Surprisingly there is much argument as to what is the basic theme of Job. There are numerous suggestions, but we will not try to unravel these here. The very fact that there are so many different opinions on this score, suggests that we should approach the book with caution, trying to let it speak for itself.

For example, on reading the first two chapters we are tempted to state that this book is about the patience of a good man under testing. Yet we are perplexed to find that in the following long debate, this idea is at best only hinted at. We have to dig deeper and watch for the signs.

So many themes have been suggested, all of which have something going for them: why do the innocent suffer? the tragedy basic to life itself, justification by faith, the incomprehensible nature of God's dealings with man, the bankruptcy of orthodoxy, even that he is a parable of suffering Israel. Perhaps something of all these elements are to be found for no one position explains the book adequately. Maybe we are wrong to look for a "theme".

However, this is not a counsel of despair. Intention there is, but we shall have to watch this develop. In order to aid this, as mentioned in the introduction, I have opted to give a number of boxes, scattered throughout the book, which seek to trace out the main points as they develop. The numbered boxes discuss basic problems and the flow of thought. It is possible to read these first before reading the commentary. But also read them alongside the text as the discussion develops.

This commentary gives three types of reading:

1. 28 boxes designed to give you a quick overview of the whole book. It is advisable, if not necessary, to read these boxes first.

2. A commentary on the text of the book. The purpose of this is to follow the thought and argument, to make it intelligible to the reader of Job.

3. Christian Perspectives are added at the end of each chapter or section. We can never treat any of the Old Testament as though Christ had never come. So, whilst not pretending to be exhaustive, I have sought to provide gentle touches to help the reader apply the thought from a Christian and modern perspective.

I have attempted to unravel Job's book by explaining the meaning of each paragraph of thought. I have made no attempt to analyse each verse, as some commentaries tend to do. This would have been laborious and fastidious. Moreover, I have touched very lightly on some passages, for example some of the speeches of the friends of Job, which are extremely repetitive. Even some of Job's speeches, e.g. chapter 12, have been touched on very lightly, and young Elihu's long-winded discourse, chapters 32–37, has been fingered with a nimble touch.

Job is a supreme example of the open-ended question. It raises controversies which demand an answer, but refuses to give a pat response. In doing so it points beyond itself, as does the whole Old Testament. The coming of Jesus Christ and his message is the only coping-stone possible for the book.

> **It is important
> to Read
> the 28 Boxes
> first**
>
> They will give you the main drift
> of the Argument of the book,
> and warn you of pitfalls.

1. Satan's violent assault on Job – Job 1–2

The book of Job is one of the most heart-searching, heart-rending books in the Bible, or for that matter any other literature.

Who was this man, Job? Probably an Edomite! A what? Well, the Edomites were a small tribe living precariously on the edge of the desert to the south east of Israel and the Dead Sea during the Old Testament period. How do we know he was an Edomite? He is said to have been from Uz, which Lamentations (4:21) places in the area of Edom. This in itself is remarkable, for the hero of this story was not an Israelite, not one who lived among the favoured people of the covenant.

Job 1:1. Even more remarkable is the fact that he is described as "blameless and upright; he feared God and shunned evil". The Lord, the covenant God of Israel, shows a genuine pride in, and affection for, Job, when he says to Satan, "Have you considered *my servant Job*? There is no one on earth like him; he is blameless and upright, a man who fears God and shuns evil." This goodness and godliness, this hatred of evil,

---

Box 1 – The Lord's true servant

Job is a servant of the LORD. 'LORD' is the covenant name for God. A 'servant' of the LORD is one who has entered into willing service for him. God has offered a special relationship of mutual trust, and this man has accepted it. He may not belong to the people of the covenant – Israel – but he has his own unique covenant with the LORD. Twice the LORD himself called him by this title, and it is of particular importance to note that at the end of the book he is still the LORD's servant (42:8). Whatever may happen between the beginning and the end, Job comes through it all triumphantly as the LORD's faithful servant. This is a first clue to the meaning of the book.

distinguishes the character of "the greatest man among all the people of the East". Wealth and godliness do not sit easily together. Wealthy people often exploit the power which affluence provides for their own ends. Not so Job, as he later demonstrates in chapter 29, a chapter well worth reading first since it sets out the character of a man whom God is happy to introduce as his friend.

Might this suggest to us that there are good people, even very good people, who do not knowingly respond to the Christian message? The men of the wisdom schools, the scribes of Israel, were conscious of this presence of God among the heathen, as is shown by the way they quote the wisdom of non-Israelites, in Proverbs 30 and 31.

1:4-5 Not that Job had an easy way with life. He was pained by the conduct of his sons, who clearly were more interested in living it up on the basis of their father's wealth. Maybe the old man wouldn't spend much on himself, but his sons were determined to spend it for him, with constant parties and discos. Job would rise early in the morning to offer sacrifices, begging the mercy of God for the sake of his sons.

Satan
1:6 From the revelry of the sons we are whisked to the heavenly court, where myriads of angels crowd surround the divine throne. Among these, "Satan also came with them". We are astonished to find Satan, the pinnacle of evil, lurking in the divine court. Perhaps we shall find many other surprises in this book. Be prepared!

He is asked what he spends his time doing, and replies that he comes from "roaming through the earth and going to and fro in it." He is the eternal tramp, with no fixed abode! That is not to despise all itinerants. Many take to this way because life has been cruel to them, and they merit our pity rather than our disdain. Others take to that life for sheer love of the freedom of the open road. But this vagabond has chosen that way of being because it suits his purpose to a 't'. He is utterly vicious in his intentions.

What shall we make of Satan? It is important to notice that his attack on Job had to be cleared with the Lord. Satan could not touch this good man, unless God gave him permission. Satan is clearly not a free agent. These chapters show us that he can do no more than God permits him to do. There is a grave danger in some Christian circles of becoming so preoccupied with the Evil One, that he is pictured as though he were almost equal to God, so that the two are locked in eternal combat. Nothing could be further from the truth. The Lord will only allow him enough rope with which to hang himself, as he so often does.

Satan's cynicism: Does Job fear God for nothing?

Satan's belief is that no one would serve God from pure motives, "for nothing". In his eyes Job only serves God for what he can get out of the relationship. He believes that all humans are basically as false and self-seeking as he is. Integrity is not a word found in his dictionary. God had richly blessed Job, so that he was a rich and powerful man. No wonder he was happy serving God.

The unbeliever can rarely believe in the integrity of the Christian man. Let a dedicated evangelist loose, and they will accuse him of seeking material gain from his preaching. The covetous, self-seeking, self-enriching Christian worker is a well-trodden theme of the media. That is not to say that this never happens, but it is rare.

Satan now proposes a "bet" with the Lord. "Let me have him! I'll strip him of everything he has, then let's see if he will not turn violently against you." Frankly, I would have expected the Lord to have defended Job and warned Satan off, but instead he hands over the unsuspecting Job to the Tormentor, even though with certain restrictions, who sets off a series of events which strip Job of everything he has:

His cattle, 1:14
His flocks and their shepherds, 1:16
His camels and their retainers, 1:17
His sons and daughters and their spouses, 1:18-19.

These four events happened in one day, from four different quarters. As one messenger brought bad news, "while he was still speaking," another messenger brought further disastrous news.

All this is set within the context of the drunken revelries of Job's ten grown children (vv.13,18), which must have heightened the feeling of guilt which the old man felt. Yet his reaction is one of humble piety. So far from cursing the Lord, he "got up and tore his robe...shaved his head... fell to the ground in worship". Here, indeed was a thoroughly godly man. Imagine coming home from church on a Sunday morning, and finding that your house, with all your precious belongings, has burnt to the ground. Would you worship God? Job did. What an incredible faith! He must surely be rated as one of the greatest believers ever. He clung tenaciously to the goodness of his God, convinced that the Lord was just as gracious in taking everything from him, as he was in giving everything to him in the past. Let us humble ourselves in the presence of such a believer, and seek to emulate his faith.

> Naked I came from my mother's womb,
>   and naked I shall depart.
> The LORD gave and the LORD has taken away;
>   may the name of the LORD be praised (v.21).

Christian Reflections

1:6-7: The expression, "roaming through the earth and going to and fro in it" is well captured in the New Living Version, where Satan says that he is "watching everything that goes on". He is ever open-eyed, seeking to destroy everyone who takes a stand for God. The apostle Peter affirms, "Be...alert. Your enemy the devil prowls around like a roaring lion, looking for someone to devour. Resist him" (I Pet. 5:8). James joins in the chorus, and exhorts us, "Resist the devil, and he will flee from you" (James 4:7). It would appear that the old lion has false teeth! However, let us admit that it doesn't always seem like that, and sometimes he appears to hold the upper hand for a long time, as in this story of Job.

How do you think that your enemy, the Devil, seeks to destroy you? Or does he? Does he need to? This beginning of the book suggests that Satan primarily intends to attack those whom God describes as his servants. Are you God's servant?

Verse 8: Satan getting clearance from the Lord is a great consolation to the believer, of whom Jesus said, "even the very hairs of your head are all numbered" (Matt. 10:30). It is true that God "brings out the starry host one by one, and calls them each by name" (Isa. 40:26), but just as surely he tots up the number of the hairs on your believing head. Satan will do nothing to you, except by the Lord's express permission, and that to achieve your Father's own purpose.

Do you think that Satan has ever overstretched himself in your own life, seeking to destroy you, but been foiled in the attempt?

Satan strikes back

Not content with having reduced Job to poverty and misery, and still unconvinced that a man can serve God with integrity, Satan decides to attack Job's physical and emotional health. He plans to reduce him to pulp, to a shivering mass of pain, fear and distrust. But once again he must seek permission from the Lord. He comes anew, measly-mouthed and drivelling, into the divine presence.

Once again, the Lord proudly points to Job's response: "he still maintains his integrity, though you incited me against him to ruin him without any reason" (2:3). The great Detractor has a further proposal. He admits that Job has not been greatly affected by the loss of possessions, but touch his body, destroy the old man's physical health, "and he will surely curse you to your face" (2:5). Once again we are astonished at the readiness with which the Lord seems to concur with the desire of Satan, who went out and "afflicted Job with painful sores from the soles of his feet to the top of his head" (v.7). Read Box 2.

Box 2 – Satan the instigator?

Superficially chapter 1 suggests that Satan was the instigator of all Job's troubles. Yet curiously this is never suggested in the following discussion of Job and his friends, and in fact Satan disappears totally from view. If there is one thing on which Job and his friends agree, it is that God is the instigator and agent of his disastrous situation. That might sound hard to swallow, but think about it.

Yes, think about it. It was not Satan who brought up the subject of Job, but God himself, on both occasions (1:8 and 2:3). God presumably did not open his mouth and put his foot in it! We cannot imagine that he ended up kicking himself for having raised the subject of Job. Never! He knew perfectly well what Satan would request. So we must agree with Job and his friends that the Lord was the instigator of his problems.

Moreover, when Satan asked to be permitted to shake Job's life to its foundations, the Lord made no effort to defend Job from his attack, and casually agreed to give him up. Clearly God intended that Job should suffer. Furthermore, that Satan's act is the Lord's act is seen from the Lord's own words after the first attack: 'You incited me against him to ruin him without any reason' (2:3). We must add to this the fact that the conclusion of the whole story clearly attributes all of Job's trials to the Lord (42:11).

Job on the refuse dump

Mankind has always had problems as to how to dispose of its waste. Towns and villages in biblical times disposed of rubbish and body waste by carrying it out to a common disposal point. From time to time this would be set alight to reduce it to ashes. Lepers and other outcasts would come here to scrounge. In times of public or personal disaster men came to sit (Isa. 47:1; Jon. 3:6), to throw dust on their heads (Ezek. 27:30), or to roll in the ashes (Jer. 6:26).

So Job is an outcast. His festering sores are disgusting to see, and people want him out of sight. Plus, his desperate situation is, in their opinion, a sure sign of God's hatred, so people must equally repudiate him. There he sits, day after day, night after night, week after week, for how long we do not know. He lives among the rotting stench of decomposing waste, knowing his children are dead, whilst his wife rejects his company; he finds some relief for his sores by scraping their itching with dirty pieces of broken pottery (2:8); young men insult him (30:1), drunks sing songs in the taverns to celebrate his downfall (30:9), they spit in his face as they pass (30:10); his skin is burned black by the blistering sun (30:30) whilst at night, so far from relief in sleep, he is haunted by frightening nightmares (7:13-14). His humble response is to say: "Shall we receive good from God, and not trouble?" (2:10).

Here is the triumph of faith in the life of a thoroughly good man. Here is the true witness to Jesus Christ. For there is no one who receives a higher accolade (1:1,8; 2:3), or can claim a loftier description of his character (ch. 29) in Scripture, than does this man Job, apart from Jesus himself. Maybe we should see him as a pale shadow of Jesus.

It is important to notice that Job knows nothing of what happened behind the scenes in heaven in chapters 1 and 2. We know, we are privileged observers of the story, sharers of a secret which Job, the hero, does not and must not know. But in his ignorance of the full facts he will experience distress and gain discernment which we will only experience at second hand.

Verses 11-13 We note in passing the coming together of three friends to support Job in his suffering. They spent a week in agonised silence, broken only by the moans and sobs of Job, echoed by his friends. We shall not pause to consider them here, but shall return to them in chapter 4.

Christians Reflections

verse 4: *The Voice of Satan.* Dr. G. Campbell Morgan once wrote a booklet with this title. He pointed out that, while the footprints and evil tricks of Satan are to be found all over the Bible, he is heard to speak only three times.

In his accusation of God to Adam, suggesting that God was mean and stingy in not allowing Adam to indulge his appetites to the full (Gen. 3). Here in Job, where he accuses man before God, of a total lack of integrity. In the Gospels, where he confronts the God-man, Jesus Christ, in the crisis encounter between the thoroughly evil and the totally good beings.

How would you say that these self-same accusations and confrontations have occurred in your own experience, or in those of others known to you?

verse 4: So you think you've got problems? Compared with Job's they must be trivial. No, I shouldn't say that. None of our problems are trivial, but, again, none of them can compare with Job. What is more, when we suffer, our sufferings are usually alleviated by numerous factors. If it is physical suffering, for example, we are seldom abandoned by our family, we are surrounded by good hospital and nursing facilities, our society does show some amount of care, rather than thrusting us out to sit on the rubbish pit. It would appear to be a custom in the Bible to give us extreme examples, in order to enable us to get some kind of perspective on our own problems.

Name some problem, physical, social or mental, which you have experienced in life, and measure it by Job's. What relief did you have that Job did not? What lesson does this bring home to you?

2. Job's Gethsemane – Chapter 3

The reader will be shocked to read chapter three. Without a word of warning the humble, believing, submissive Job has become a bitter rebel. The hero has fallen! God's 'bet' on his 'horse' has failed! Job crashes in despair.

There have not lacked those Bible students who have decided that these two pictures of Job are mutually inconsistent, that these writings come from different hands, who have different conceptions of how Job would have reacted, one seeing him as submissive, trusting, believing; the other seeing him as a rebel who is angered by the way God has permitted such a disaster into his life.

Box 3 – Did God lose his 'bet' on Job?

Could it be that this 'wager' between God and Satan, elaborated in chapters 1 and 2, is the key to the book's interpretation? It is natural to think that an author will indicate his theme at the beginning of the book. The reader instinctively feels that this is the theme. Indeed, chapter 3 almost makes us feel that God has lost the bet, his horse has fallen at the first hurdle! But we must tread carefully.

It's curious that in the very long discussion of the problem, chapters 3 to 31, this theme never enters into it. Indeed, Job never cursed God, and he clung tenaciously to the belief that the Lord is ultimately on his side. In this he came out victorious by the end of the book, so that the Lord proved his point, that Job did love and serve him 'for nothing'. So the answer to our question is, that, though the reader may be tempted in chapter 3, and on several other occasions, to think that Job has gone overboard in his highly emotional responses, in reality he has not. But only by reading the whole book can we be assured of that. We might at times feel as though Job has blown a gasket, and only the book as a whole can convince us otherwise. We shall see.

Are these two pictures of Job contradictory? Not at all. It reminds us of the account of Elijah defying hundreds of prophets of Baal, calling fire down from heaven, and seeing a whole people turn back to God. Here, indeed, was a man of power, of might, of life. Yet in the very next scene he is running for his life from the threats of Jezebel, and throws himself under a tree and contemplates suicide! (I Kings 18-19). God then ministers to his weakness, for his servant has suffered burn-out in the midst of a seemingly victorious fight.

In Job's case his initial supercharged faith leads to the assertion of complete acceptance of God's will in chapter 2. But this is followed by a week on the rubbish tip, weeping and moaning his terrible distress, accompanied by the weeping of his friends, and the scorn of his fellow-citizens. They say a week is a long time in politics, how much more in Job's condition. A week to agonize in total misery. For a week Job wept without saying a coherent word. But what must have been the multitude of thoughts which crashed through his brain? Why? Why me? What have I done to deserve this? His mood must have fluctuated several times a day between the humble submission to the will of God, displayed in chapters 1 and 2, and anger at the seeming injustice of his suffering. Even within his recorded speeches his mood fluctuates violently between utter despair and soaring hope.

What is more, we must hear Job out. We must not react to one chapter, we must read the whole before we can determine the intention of the parts. The section will then fit into the mosaic of the whole, and each will be seen to be comprehensible.

The man who cursed his birth-day – read 3:1-10
Birthdays for us are an annual cause of celebration, for they remind us of our birth. In biblical days, when a girl was born it was announced in hushed tones, but when a boy was born it was a cause for jubilation. So here, at his birth, the cry went up around the neighbourhood, and among his family, "It's a boy!" (v.3). But for Job the cry of joy has become the scream of pain.

From the depths of pain and despair he curses the day he

was born. He wishes that it could be erased from the calendar, a non-day. If that day had earlier been blotted out, Job would never have been born, and he thinks that would be a better condition than the present one. His former life, of material fortune, of high place in society, of sweet enjoyment, in which "my path was drenched with cream and the rock poured out for me streams of olive oil" (29:6), has faded from memory as the present reality dominates his every thought.

Job heaps line upon line, conjuring up to his imagination all the possible forces which might have enabled that day not to have existed. Since that day could not be blotted from the calendar, Job utters his own curse upon it, "May those who curse days curse that day" (v.8). Enchanters had in biblical days the supposed power to curse particular days, making them unlucky. In particular the professional mourners at a funeral would curse the day of the funeral person's death. Job would rather they cursed his birth-day, than that of his coming death. He feels that his birth-day was not one of good fortune, being introduced to the joys of life, but one which held in store for several decades all his present suffering. Such is his bitterness of soul.

There is a striking similarity between this passage and that of another sufferer (Jer. 20:14-18). Jeremiah had recently been beaten up and put in the stocks for 24 hours by the temple police and had suffered deep hatred from the general public. Yet he was still able to go about his normal business, even to buy property (ch. 32). Job's sufferings are total. If ever there was a man entitled to rebel against life's harsh realities, it was Job.

Once again we turn to our own suffering. It may be that protest is a legitimate part of all suffering. For some it may be possible to stifle the "Why?" (are they brain dead?) but for most of us this is impossible. And the "Why me?" may in the long-run be constructive, as it was for Job. God, however, may be long in replying to our question, so that we shall have to stick with it, as Job did.

Longing for death – read 3:11-19

Since it is not possible for his birth-day to be cursed with hindsight, Job wishes that he could have been still-born. Death would have been eminently preferable to life. Here we cannot but feel that he has the whole matter out of focus. Up till this terrible week, he had experienced a very happy, peaceful and fruitful life (which chapter 29 expounds in detail). But when we are plunged into a disaster like his, everything gets out of perspective. Our world, like his, comes tumbling down. We want to scream at the whole world.

The husband of a lady I know died whilst on a family holiday, suddenly, unexpectedly. As she watched people going past her house to work in the following days, she wanted to scream at them to stop doing these normal things. Didn't they know that her husband had died? We all feel like this when disaster strikes, and it is an indication of the way we make the world revolve around us, so that when our life stops, we want everyone else to stop with us.

This passage raises an interesting question about life after death. It is a striking fact that the Old Testament has little to say about this, though other peoples around them, e.g. the Egyptians, were intensely preoccupied with the subject. The biblical writers could not have been ignorant of this, yet they chose to downplay it. Why? Perhaps because they were conscious that everything the nations affirmed about that state was speculative, and often farcical. For Job the longing for death is the anticipation that essentially it offers a place where "the wicked cease from turmoil, and there the weary are at rest" (v.17). In contrast with the present harsh realities it will be a place of peace and rest.

Note also that there is here "the democracy of death", where kings, cabinet ministers and billionaires rest alongside the wicked, the weary, the captives and the slave drivers.

Why is life given to those in misery? – read 3:20-26

Job's experience causes him to reach out beyond his own sufferings, to ask questions about the experience of humans in general. This becomes, as the story develops, an extremely important part of his thinking. The sufferer, whose life is unceasing pain and misery, longs for death, but an apparently compassionate God denies it to him, indeed he has "hedged him in", allowing him no escape route out of his misery.

It is here crucial for us to understand that Job's whole conception of God has taken a very rude knock. He had spent his whole life, he was now approaching 'retirement' years, in the firm belief that if one lives a good life God is certain to bless him, and this had been his daily experience for decades before this terrible tragedy struck him. The very nature of the Lord, the covenant God of grace, seemed to hang in the balance now.

But the God whom he now meets wears a different face. His smile has turned to a frown or, worse, a scowl, and Job knows no reason to justify this. It adds deep mental agony to the physical and social distress he already experiences. I suspect that we all go through this to some degree when we suffer. Augustine it was who declared that either God could relieve suffering but will not, or would like to relieve suffering but cannot. Augustine's little riddle is too simplistic for the author of this book. Job will plumb the depths of suffering, both in himself, and in the world in general.

The final thing to notice in this chapter is the unexpected statement in verse 25: "What I feared has come upon me; what I dreaded has happened to me." Clearly in the midst of a prosperous, powerful and happy life there had lurked a hidden anxiety, that all of this might one day be lost, and that he might be reduced to poverty and misery. It is sometimes observed by the rich that the poor spend their time dreaming of being rich, which may well be true, as our modern fascination for getting rich quick, e.g. the lottery or "Who Wants To Be a Millionaire", proves to be true. Yet I suggest that very often the rich have horrific dreams of one day becoming poor, and the dreams of the poor are sweeter than the nightmares of the rich!

The cry of this chapter, the agonised despair of life, the longing for non-existence, is important for the whole book, since it sets the basic scene on which all later argument will be based. It is the shock of these initial words of Job which set his friends recoiling in anger at his gall in attacking God in this way.

Christian Reflections

Chapter 3: Throughout this chapter Job flings into the air, into the face of his friends, into God's face, into our faces, a multitude of questions. Read all the "Why.....s" in this chapter. If you are shocked by what he says, I beg you not to judge him harshly. **How would you/do you react in similar situations?** Our suffering is minimal in comparison with his. Only such who have suffered as he did have a right to judge his reactions.

Verse 25: "What I feared has come upon me." We too fear insecurity. Our modern financial security systems – pensions, insurances for every imaginable type of problem, mortgages, annuities, etc., reflect the same fears, yet these securities are all fleeting. They can disappear in no time if and when the system goes wrong. The Christian needs to keep constantly before him the exhortations of Jesus against the sin of worry (Matt. 6:25-34); as also those of Paul: "Do not be anxious about anything, but in everything, by prayer and petition, with thanksgiving, present your requests to God. And [in consequence] the peace of God, which transcends all understanding, will guard your hearts and your minds in Christ Jesus" (Phil. 4:6,7).
   What fear of the future affects you at present? How much does it affect you? What are you doing about it, physically, financially, but above all spiritually (i.e. in a godly manner)?

Verse 26: **Job's Gethsemane?** Surely the title is legitimate. Our Lord longed, that if at all possible, the cup of suffering might be taken from him. The writer of Hebrews affirms that "in the days of Jesus' life on earth, he offered up prayers and petitions with loud cries and tears" (5:7). He did not contemplate suffering and death with tranquillity. It rocked his boat, as it did Job's. The difference comes between Job's defiant spirit and Jesus' response of humble submission to the will of his Father.

Consider these two alternatives in the face of suffering –
defiant spirit or humble submission. Which would best
characterise your own response. Which is the best way? Are
they mutually contradictory? See Paul's way in 2
Corinthians 12:7-10.

3. Eliphaz' first discourse – chapters 4–5

When Job, after a week of silence, opened his mouth, what
would his friends have expected him to say? We shall never
know, but one thing is certain, they never expected him to
violently curse the day of his birth. They were clearly shocked.
Eliphaz is the first to react, and his speech is very important.
The other speeches of the friends only echo or expand on this.

Box 4 – Job's friends

We must respect Job's friends. They are not, as we might
be tempted to think, insincere. Whilst the local people,
who had benefitted so much from Job's wisdom and
wealth, had rejected him, they came from long distances
and sat down to share his grief in silence for a whole week
(2:11-13). This was friendship of the highest order. They
are initially presented in a favourable light, sensitive and
compassionate to Job. Their whole intention was to
sympathise with him and to comfort him.

What is more, they really were good, earnest and
religious men. Their speeches were well-meaning and
often quite striking, and were designed to bring comfort
to Job. Yet ironically their 'comfort' proved a constant
irritation to our hero. Indeed, in the light of their later
words and actions, their period of silence may be seen as
their finest hour. We shall need to keep a sharp eye on
their teaching, and its deficiencies, its mixture of truth
and error.

Eliphaz' knee-jerk reaction – read chapter 4

Eliphaz was a native of Teman, a town of the Arabian desert. He has clearly been stung by Job's terrible, destructive cry in chapter 3. It must have sent shivers down his spine, for in his eyes, to curse the day of your birth lays the blame on the One who caused you to be born. Yet he is every bit a gentleman, and begins by being patient and gracious (v.2). He recognizes that Job has been a help to many people during his life, and this agrees with chapter 29, where he is described in such terms as would make him the cream of Old Testament saints. But, Eliphaz points out, you have not been so quick to apply your remedies to your own sickness (vv. 5f).

Even so, he does not accuse Job of any sin, recognising that his life has been godly and blameless (v.6). Indeed, in his cry to God he should be able to appeal through the merit gained by his good life. He does not accuse Job of any sin, yet implicitly he recognises that there is something wrong, something of which perhaps Job himself is unaware.

After the brief opening, the affirmation of verse 7 represents the basic argument of Eliphaz, Bildad and Zophar: **Who being innocent ever perished?** In one form or another they will drive home this sure conviction. In 2:11 we learn that they had met together before approaching Job, and no doubt they then agreed to a common strategy for 'comforting' Job. It was to get him to admit to something wrong in his life. There is, says Eliphaz, a common, divinely-appointed, unalterable law built into the order of things – "those who plough evil and those who sow trouble reap it" (v.8). It follows that since Job has reaped trouble, there must be some evil in his life. Politely Eliphaz says this indirectly, allowing Job to make his own conclusions.

The fascination of this concept, a God who hands out reward and punishment according to merit, has dominated religious thinking, and invaded every form of Christianity over the centuries. Compare the judgment of Jesus ben Sirach, a Jewish wise man writing hundreds of years after Job and 150 years before Christ: *"Consider the past generations and see; was*

Box 5 – Who, being innocent, has ever perished? 4:7
This statement by Eliphaz is the basic position of Job's
friends. During the following dialogue they stuck to this line
through thick and thin. Retribution, reward and punishments,
lie at the heart of the order of things in a just world ordered
by a just God, in their view. Are they right? There are ample
Scriptures to suggest that God blesses those who do right,
and punishes those who do wrong. Listen to the Proverbs:
'No harm befalls the righteous, but the wicked have their fill
of trouble' (12:21); 'The fear of the LORD leads to life; then
one rests content untouched by trouble' (19:23).

Yet it is not the whole truth. We can see two vitally
different positions operating among thinkers in the Old
Testament. On the one hand, those who hold this basic
theory, on the other, those who suggest that life is far too
complex to admit such an easy explanation. A good
example of the former is Psalm 37 with its constant
affirmation that 'evil men will be cut off, but those who
hope in the LORD will inherit the land' (v. 9). Read the
whole psalm. Yes, the psalmist in Psalm 73 feels that often
the contrary is true: '*I envied the arrogant when I saw the
prosperity of the wicked.... This is what the wicked are
like – always carefree, they increase in wealth... [in
contrast] all day long I have been plagued; I have been
punished every morning*' (vv. 3-14). Like Job, the more
he tried to understand this, 'it was oppressive to me...'

anyone who trusted in the Lord ever disappointed? Was anyone
who stood firm in the fear of Him ever deserted? Did he ever
neglect anyone who prayed to him?*" To each of his questions
ben Sirach expects an emphatic 'Never!' from his reader.
Ecclesiasticus 2:10

A Bible ghost-story – read 4:12-21

Eliphaz represents the mentality of conclusions based on religious experience. He tells of a frightening dream he had had many years before. "A spirit glided past my face, and the hair on my body stood on end" (v.15). We need not doubt the genuineness of his experience, but the message conveyed by the whispering voice sounds rather unexceptional: "Can a mortal be more righteous than God? Can a man be more pure than his Maker?" Job would not have doubted that these questions held a large element of truth. Since God is infinitely superior to the creature he has made, it is not possible for a human to dispute his own fate. Eliphaz' vision grounded the negative on man's total insignificance when confronted by his Maker.

It is highly probable that Eliphaz' experience was genuine, a gift of God's grace. At some time in his life he had needed to learn that lesson, and God drove it home to him in this nightmare. The statement is true. We all stand before God as fragile, mortal and faulty. Eliphaz includes even the heavenly hosts with being an integral part of the fallenness of creation (v.18). Since the whole created order is tainted with imperfection, Job must stand with it and acknowledge that he is part of it.

Mysterium tremendum et fascinans

This Latin phrase means that when we encounter God we are both scared and fascinated. Our first instinct is to run, to take cover, to hide (Ps. 139:5-12), but our next should be to say, with the same psalmist, "Search me, O God, and know my heart..." (v. 23). When Isaiah saw the Lord he cried, "I am ruined", but when the Lord offers him the opportunity of service, his reply was immediate, "Here am I. Send me" (Isa. 6:5-8). The trouble with Eliphaz is that he had experienced the tremendous mystery, but he had never been fascinated by it, never been drawn to it, never fallen in love with God. His God knew no mercy. He simply dished out rewards according to merit.

Although his religious experience may have been genuine,

and what he says may be true in itself, yet he never got beyond
this early experience, this basic truth. It became a measuring
stick by which he gauged and weighed everybody. This is always
a danger for us. We tend to measure others by the ruler of our
own experience, and within the limitations of our knowledge.
To some extent this may be necessary, but once it becomes
rigid and inflexible, once we are not able to listen to other ways
of seeing things, we are likely to become hard and
unapproachable, locked up in the narrow confines of our own
experience.

Eliphaz does not accuse Job directly of sin. He expects Job
to draw that conclusion for himself. The trouble was that the
very general truth which he proclaims has little bearing on the
case of Job. It must be remembered that we, the readers, have
had the privilege, in chapters 1–2, of a behind-the-curtains view
of what lay behind Job's sufferings, a view which has been
denied to Job or his friends. We have been forewarned of Job's
absolute integrity, of which Eliphaz is completely ignorant.

Man is born to trouble – read 5:1-7
Eliphaz continues to press his case, though it now becomes
somewhat more pointed. In verse 1 he taunts Job. Job has cried
out in chapter 3, but who does he expect to answer his cry? His
appeal is against God, but there is none of "the holy ones"
(angels) who will hear, receive or present his complaint. All
creation is on God's side against Job, which, of course, means
on Eliphaz' side, since he has taken on the role of the wise,
divinely-appointed counsellor.

Eliphaz was clearly stung by Job's heartfelt cry of rebellion
against the lot life had dealt him, and he now accuses Job, again
by innuendo rather than by direct statement, of being riddled
by resentment (v.2). Job has shown himself, by his display of
bad temper, to have fallen into folly, to be in danger of becoming
a fool. The phrase, 'the simple', which lies parallel to 'fool' in
this verse, is very important in the book of Proverbs. In that
book it means young men who are as yet unformed as to the

way they will take in life. The simple may very easily become
fools if they go the way of evil. Again, implicitly, Job, by his
cries in chapter 3, has entered on the slippery slope of madness.
Eliphaz would have said today that his words were verbal
garbage!

Once you are on that route you are in grave danger of total
ruin. An impatient fool will only bring upon himself greater
disaster, leading eventually to his total destruction, Eliphaz
argues. Once again he appeals to experience to prove his point.
He has seen a fool apparently getting away with it, but disaster
has suddenly struck and he has lost the lot, house and home,
family and children, property, indeed everything (vv. 3-5). This
must have sounded to Job too near to home to have encouraged
him!

Indeed, says Eliphaz, this is an inflexible law of the divinely-
ordered universe (vv. 6-7). Suffering and trouble are not
something from outside, but result from causes latent in human
nature. Man through his inclination to evil creates trouble for
himself "as surely as sparks fly upward" (v.7).

If it were I... – read 5:8-27

Eliphaz is a moraliser. In many ways his attacks on Job are a
self-justification, a self-indulgence. By implication he is morally
superior to Job, and therefore can give himself the luxury of
delivering a sermon. He is quite sure that were their roles
reversed he would be an example to all of the way to deal with
suffering. He would not stomp his feet angrily, as Job had, but
would lay his case humbly before God, knowing that from him
he would receive grace and favour (v.8).

His sermon is quite eloquent, one of the finest passages in
the book. He makes two points. First, God works in sovereign
power, but always in perfect goodness and justice (vv. 9-16).
You should trust God without asking questions, for God knows
what he is doing. Our need is not to question, but to marvel at
his works. Trust God without asking questions. Secondly, if
Job will but desist from bad temper at God's dealings with him,

which is only divine discipline, he will be quickly restored and richly blessed (vv.17-26).

Suffering to Eliphaz is always disciplinary, and is in fact a divinely appointed blessing: cp. Proverbs 3:11f. and Hebrews 12:5-11. It is divine discipline, painful, but necessary and beneficial. Once the distress has had its way in correcting Job, life will be all sunshine once more. By implication, Job is guilty, and he must weather the storm of divine severity, knowing that though God wounds, "he also binds up; he injures, but his hands also heal" (v.18).

Warming to his subject, Eliphaz treats Job to a dream picture of his restored state (vv.19-26). He will experience secure divine protection from all possible calamities, his home and property will be restored to him, he will have many children, and, most blessed of all, he will live long and at peace with the world and with God. No brighter prospect in this world could have been offered to our hero.

How painful are honest words! See 6:25
This is Job's comment on Eliphaz' speech (6:25). He does not refute all that the wise man says. There are many things of value in his speech. He sometimes touches on, even expounds, great truths.

Yet his last words gave the game away: "We have examined this, and it is true. So hear it and apply it to yourself" (v.27). This is the voice of the moralizer. He pontificates. 'Es más Papa que el Papa!' say the Spanish – he is more Pope than the Pope himself! He has had his experience of God and is determined to measure the world by it. He has sorted out his 'truth' and uses it as a yardstick to measure everything. He will pour everyone into his own mould, and if they don't fit, there must be something gravely wrong. So Job's duty, his wisdom, is to listen attentively, then apply these exhortations in their entirety to his own case. Eliphaz' sermon is intended to comprehend the whole truth. He certainly felt at this point that his argument was irrefutable, that he had shut Job up!

However, his doctrine is by no means certain. He abounds in universal ideas, but is unable to consider the possibility of other explanations. He holds one rigid theory of God's dealings with man, and uses it to lecture Job. Above all, it never occurs to him to put his hand around Job's shoulder, to listen to his sobbing voice, to show him compassion. The trouble is that he does not understand that Job's protest embodies his distress, and in this there is no place for interminable, abstract teaching about God and his ways with man, which is all Eliphaz has to offer.

The apostle Paul quoted directly from this sermon in I Corinthians 3:19. Clearly in some sense there is in his sermon the word of God. Paul uses this one expression (v.13) to rebuke the arrogant intellectuals who refuse the message of the Cross. Any of the friends' statements in this book may hold much truth, but this does not endorse the way they are being applied to Job.

Christian Reflections

Verse 7: When the disciples asked Jesus concerning a man born blind, *"Rabbi, who sinned, this man or his parents, that he was born blind?"* (John 9:1-2), they showed that they too had not learned the lesson of Job. Like many voices today, they lived in a world of cause and effect. Here you see an effect – a man born blind. Your logic says, there must be a clearly intelligible cause lying behind this visible event. There are those today, who, if someone is prayed for and doesn't immediately show signs of healing, will assume, and even say, that there is some hidden sin in the sufferer's life! Is it not incredible that we still have not learned from Job?

Can you relate some experience in your life, or in that of someone known to you where this concept has shown itself today? Confronted with the same mentality now, how would you respond?

Chapters 4-5: Eliphaz' speech greatly increased Job's distress and agony. Eliphaz thought he was doing good, and he will go on to speak of the 'comfort' his words should bring to Job, although we soon see that he has the contrary effect.

Can you recall similar attempts to console the suffering, which have only deepened the agony and distress of the sufferer? How might you have righted the wrong done by bad counselling?

4. Job's reply to Eliphaz – Chapters 6–7

These two chapters divide easily and naturally into two parts. In the first, Job reacts to Eliphaz' speech; in the second, he reflects more profoundly on his terrible lot, turning then to God in prayer.

Although chapter 6 is a reaction to Eliphaz, it is important to notice that Job does not address Eliphaz directly, and that he is plainly including the other friends, Bildad and Zophar. Clearly during the speech they will have indicated their approval of everything Eliphaz had said with angrily-flashing eyes, nodding heads, gestures, grunts and murmurs of approval. So Job is left in no doubt that the speech has their full consent.

Job defends his "resentment" – read 6:1-7
Translators, for a variety of reasons, do not render words in the same way every time they occur. Yet at times the connection with a previous word used may be important, and the failure to show this in translation may leave the reader in ignorance of what is really being said. In 5:2 Eliphaz had accused Job of *ka'as,* 'resentment'. This had clearly stung Job, and he picks it up in his reply, where NIV's "anguish" *(ka'as)* is the same word as "resentment" in 5:2. Eliphaz had never suffered as Job had, and was, therefore, totally incapable of understanding his complaint. Job proceeds to admit (3b) that he may have over-stepped the limits in chapter 3. He had been impetuous, but he had good reason to be. If his misery were placed on scales, all the sands on the ocean sea shores of the world wouldn't outweigh it!

Box 6 – God, by any other name?

There is a striking difference in this book with respect to the divine name. In the first two chapters, God is 'the LORD', the covenant name, the name of grace and love. It is at first astonishing to find that this name is never used in the dialogue between Job and his friends. Instead God is called Elohim, the common name for God in the ancient world. It sounds cold and distant, as does the other name which is used extensively, Shaddai, the Almighty (6:4). Of the 48 times Shaddai appears in the Old Testament, 31 are here in Job. Yet when God finally speaks at the end of the story, we see God referred to exclusively with the covenant name.

How do we explain this change? The early part, and the latter part, of the book represent God as he has made himself known to Job throughout his life. He has known God as the LORD, the lover of his soul, the One who has heaped blessing on his life, enriching and honouring him as his servant. But in these sufferings he meets God by another name, by another face, in another form.

Now it is precisely this change in God which drives him to madness. God's love and blessing has been exchanged for apparent wrath and curse. For Job the situation is intolerable. For his friends, nothing has changed, the same fixed laws determine every man's relationship with God. For Job, everything has changed. He is perplexed, he is distraught, he is incoherent. Can this be the same God? Yet Job can believe in no other god, he can look for no other god. In his suffering he meets this alien God, yet is convinced he deals with the same God who had for decades ministered to him so lovingly, so kindly.

How shall he reconcile these two realities, these two pictures of God? This is the deep agony of Job. Can he cling to the early knowledge of God in the present distress?

The arrows of the Almighty are in me,
my spirit drinks in their poison

What Job now affirmed, which profoundly added to his mental distress, was that he was persuaded that **God was entirely responsible for all that he suffered** (v.4). God is a brutal hunter (v.4), unscrupulous in his choice of weapons. He rains poisonous arrows into his victim's body and soul. Remember that Job knows nothing of intermediaries – "Satan" of chapters 1–2. We have been privileged to see behind the curtain, but these scenes in heaven were never revealed to Job or his friends, and in one thing they concur – *God is the author of Job's sufferings*. Take particular notice here of what is said in Box 6. Job is seeing and experiencing God in a different way than the God of kindness and blessing which he had always previously known. As the argument develops we shall see that Job returns to this theme again and again. So it is not to be treated as a forgivable one-off remark.

More to the point, how did Job's friends react? They agree with Job that God is the author of his pain. But the shocking implication of his remark was that God was unfair, totally unscrupulous in what he was doing. For Eliphaz, Bildad and Zophar this was nothing less than blasphemy. Can't you see their eyes blazing in anger, their heads shaking in unbelief.

In the light of such intense distress, the sermons which the friends proffer him are "tasteless food" (vv. 6,7).

Job cries for relief – read 6:8-10

Job turns from argument and returns to his cry of chapter 3. There he had desired never to have been born, here he longs to be cut off immediately from life. What a terrible cry is this! *"Oh that I might have my request, that God would grant what I hope for, that God would be willing to crush me, to let loose his hand and cut me off!"* He wants God to kill him! Many a sufferer has reached this point, longing for death to bring relief to terrible suffering.

It is interesting to note that death was the one factor which

Satan was prohibited from inflicting on Job (2:6). Therefore, even God's hands are tied from giving to Job this last recourse. Many a sufferer must have breathed such a prayer to their Maker. Perhaps, like Job, the Almighty has good reasons for not agreeing to the request.

If verse 4 has introduced us to an important thread of Job's thought, another line is here introduced: the conviction of his innocence (v.10). He will voice this louder as time goes on. It is a fixed point of reference, his one consolation in the midst of incredible suffering. This is worth some reflection, "my joy in unrelenting pain". In the coming days and nights of torment, when everything seems black and devastating, Job clings to this conviction: he has done nothing to merit this suffering, he has not denied God's word, his covenant with the Lord.

'Does God think that I am a superman, that he subjects me so?' (vv.11-13). By now Job's suffering had undermined his physical strength. He desperately feels his strength drooping, and he stares death in the face, having no hope, nor any prospect for the future. Why then does God subject him to this torture?

The barrenness of Job's friends' 'comfort' – read 6:14-23
Job now turns his full guns on his friends. So far from comforting him, they have been miserable failures. Considering this is after only one speech, chapters 4–5, this is strong language from Job, but he seems to sense that they have agreed as to their line of attack, and will stick to it to the end. Which is, in fact, what they did.

What does one ask of a friend? Devotion. The word for devotion is a rich one in the Old Testament. It is loyal love, love based on a relationship of mutual respect and trust. This is the least a man in Job's position could expect of them. This ought to apply even when he seems to be in the wrong. Eliphaz had said that Job's "piety" should be his confidence (4:6). Job picks up the Hebrew word and says that even if he has apparently abandoned this "fear of the Almighty", he ought still to retain his friends' compassion. That is what friendship is all about.

In contrast his friends are like the 'wadis' (vv. 15-21). These river beds in the hill country are dry most of the year, but when rain comes they are filled with torrents of water. But therein lies their problem. In the scorching heat of summer, precisely when you desperately look for water, they are bone dry, and you go away frustrated and despairing. Yet they have water in abundance when you least need them. That is the best illustration of his friends' so-called 'comfort', *"...fickle as a torrent, as the course of a seasonal stream"* (Jerusalem Bible).

Verse 21 affirms that there is fear in the friends' minds in the face of suffering. Is this not true for ourselves? Pain is not easy to confront, especially for those who have experienced little of it. Perhaps coming face-to-face with it makes us realise our own weakness, our insecurity. Hurting people often feel like the psalmist in his cry, "I looked for sympathy, but there was none, for comforters, but I found none" (Ps. 69:20).

Job has, in fact, never asked them for anything more than the simple hand of kindness, of brotherly love, but in this they have been a miserable failure.

Job asks for evidence before he is condemned – read 6:24-30
We take another important step forward with this passage. Job asks for evidence that he has committed some wrong. Apart from such evidence the arguments of his friends are without weight. If they cannot produce evidence of his sin he cannot be suffering for having denied the Lord. On the other hand, their attacks are only evidence of hardheartedness, and show a calloused mentality (v.27). Embittered, he pours contempt on their claim to possess the high moral ground: "You would even cast lots for the fatherless and barter away your friend." Perhaps he goes over the top here.

Job is utterly convinced of his own innocence. Follow his line of thought through his whole argument (6:10, 29; 9:15, 20; 10:7; 12:4,16f.; 23:12; 27:1-6). If you will only show me my sin, my suffering will be bearable!

He begs them to rethink the whole matter, for whilst for them

Box 7 – Rethinking, three steps forward.
In chapter 6 we discover three new aspects of Job's thought as he wrestles with his pain:
   • God is the author and executor of his pain (v.4)
   • He is utterly convinced of his own innocence (v.10)
   • He invites his friends to show him in what he has done wrong (v. 24)

These three factors become very important as Job's thinking develops. Remember that he will have held the same idea as his friends, before his disaster. The universe is run, or ought to run, on the basis of the law of retribution. He can no longer see things so simplistically. In his agony he is forced to rethink everything he had been taught and believed. His friends refuse to accompany him on this wild venture.

it is just an argument, for him it is a question of personal integrity: "Relent, do not be unjust; reconsider, for my integrity is at stake" (v.29). Job's defiance will not, however, produce results, for they will not specify any specific sin during the next 16 chapters. Only when Eliphaz comes to the end of his tether, does he fling accusations of wrong against Job (ch. 22), but by then we know that these are the slanders of a desperate man, who has lost all other grounds of argument.

Christian Reflections

Verse 2: Many of us are called upon to counsel those who suffer, from time to time. We have no professional training, yet nearness to the sufferer means we are in a position to help – or hinder! Sometimes the sufferer blurts out thoughts which may well shock us, thoughts we never imagined possible from this person. At such times it is heartless cruelty to confront them with

accusations such as Eliphaz did. Often there is no better reaction
than to button our lip and allow the suffering person to blast
off.

**Discuss or reflect on some experience where you have
heard sufferers blow their gasket with God. How have you
reacted? What reaction would you take in future?**

Verses 4-5: "All God's terrors are arrayed against me. Don't I
have a right to complain?" How do you react to this suggestion?
Was God responsible, or was it Satan? Note – it was God who
brought up the subject of Job's righteous life (1:8). Presumably
had he not done so, Satan would not have asked leave to test
Job. Did God bungle? Surely not. What then was God's purpose?
Was Job a sort of human guinea-pig, reduced to abject misery
in order that the Almighty might get his point across over against
Satan's cynicism?

**These questions raise serious problems with the manner
in which we think of God's dealings with us. Think of their
implications for your own life. Are they ever true?**

6:8-9: "O that God...would crush me". Had God granted Job's
request, he would have denied him the high favour of
collaboration with God. Much of God's purpose in his suffering
had to do with learning, understanding God's ways. Had God
conceded his request and killed him, he would have lost this
privilege. We too are called on to hang in there, confident in the
knowledge that there is some explanation, and that when it
comes, we shall thank God that he did not give us our request
(Campbell-Morgan).

**What learning privilege might there be in human
suffering? It will be enormously helpful here to look at what
James says in James 1:2-3. See also Paul in Romans 5:3-5.**

5. Job refuses to stop complaining – Chapter 7

In chapter 6 he has been speaking to his friends. In 7:1-5 he speaks to himself, then, in verses 6-10, to God. He turns from argument to meditation on God's ways and man's lot. His old creed has been destroyed, but the living faith within him insisted in putting out new shoots. He has lost his platitudes and clichés, but if his old theology has gone, something else must replace it.

Job sees himself as a representative of suffering humanity – read 7:1-5

He raises his voice to *protest* against the aggressive character of God's treatment of man. What was true of Job in particular is true of man in general. In life, human beings find themselves condemned to a few years of hard labour. Like a soldier, they long for demob; like a slave they long for nightfall. Job sees himself as a representative of suffering humanity. He does not

---

Box 8 – Why is life so hard? Why do people suffer?
This translation of Job 7:1 is taken from the Contemporary English Version. It captures the essence of his meaning. Do we have here the meaning of the book of Job? That the book is about suffering nobody doubts, that it is about the questions posed here is often assumed. Is the narrator of this story asking, Why do the innocent suffer? Is this the theme of the book of Job?

I have known not a few people struck by disaster who reached for this book, with the presumption that here they would find an answer to their agonized questions. It has always worried me, because if this is the basic question of the book, the answer to the question does not lie on the surface, if it is here at all. As a result these people have often gone away from Job even more confused and sometimes distressed. The book offers no simple answers to these profoundly disturbing questions.

pursue this question here, but later in the book he will return to it in detail.

This is an important characteristic of the book. Job is immersed in his own terrible problems, yet he does not remain there. They are the occasion for asking penetrating questions about man's lot on earth.

Verses 2-6 Job's miserable condition embodies and proves the prior statement. From the plight of mankind Job quickly returns to the particulars of his own situation, giving us a vivid picture of his physical suffering. It is so easy in reading the argument between Job and his friends to imagine that we are in a debating hall. But we are not. We are still on the rubbish heap, and we must never lose sight of it. The debate may seem merely argumentative, but not for a moment must we forget that our hero is sitting in the midst of filth and stench. There are no health services for society's reject (v.5). His wounds seem temporarily to heal, but the scabs break open again and throw out pus.

Night time may provide rest for the slave, but for Job there is none. Night after night he tosses and turns. How long was he in this condition? Little hint is given, but verse 3 makes mention of 'months'. Jewish tradition said that it lasted for seven years. Certainly it must have been for a significant period of time.

Job's first prayer – read 7:6-10
Verse 7 For the first time Job turns to prayer – a pitiful appeal to God. His cry, "Remember, O God..." is often heard in the Old Testament. The person in pain would call on God to remember his former goodness and good will, to treat him as he would have in the past. If we are sensitive we shall hear Job's voice choking in this agonised cry. The God of grace, the God with whom he has walked for so very long (see Box 6), has disappeared from view. Our hero invokes his return, though it seems to him that this is a futile prayer, since, "my eyes will never see happiness again."

It is the awful finality of what is happening to him that appals

Job. It is not that death in itself is frightening. It is the long, slippery slope whereby he slides into it that scares him. This is so often true when we face pain, so that the modern solution is the way of euthanasia. For Job there is no such option, though his whole being shrinks from the prospect of prolonged suffering.

And death itself – there is such a terrible finality about death (vv.8-10). But this thought stirs up another. When Job is wiped out, God will come looking for him, as he used to in times past, but then it will be too late. This introduces us to a strange fracture, an apparent contradiction, in Job's thinking. At the present he experiences that other face of God, apparently angry, destructive, yes, perhaps even, cruel. Yet he is convinced that the old God is still there behind the present face. One day this God of love will come looking for him again, but by then it will be too late, for Job will be no more.

It may be difficult for the Christian reader to understand what the Old Testament says, or perhaps better, doesn't say, about death. It often seems to view death as something frightening. Thus the psalmist complains, "I am set apart with the dead... whom you remember no more, who are cut off from your care" (Ps. 88:5). Some have concluded from this and other references that the Israelites did not believe in life after death, but this is highly improbable, given the fact that all nations around them made much of the subject, e.g. the pyramids and mummies of the Egyptians. Pre-Israelite tombs in Israel show that numerous artifacts were included for the loved one's after-life.

Can it be that the Israelites turned with distaste from the extraordinary preoccupation with death and the after-life, to emphasise that their God was the God of the now, of life on earth?

I will not shut up! – read 7:11-21
Job opens his heart to God, even though his friends might consider his talk blasphemous. These are among his bitterest words! Eliphaz has said in effect that Job should shut his mouth

and humbly accept his sufferings from the hand of God, since
he can be assured that God always acts in justice. Job here takes
the important decision to reject this suggestion. And we must
be grateful that he did, or we would not have this book to
captivate us and make us think more deeply of human suffering
and divine will.

Eliphaz has accused him of 'resentment' (5:2); Job feels he
has every right to be resentful, and that it is necessary for God
to hear his complaint. So he takes the decision to give free rein
to his anger. How often do we feel shocked when sufferers
express themselves in this manner? We are unable to handle
this kind of situation, perhaps even shocked by it. In so doing
we are joining the company of the 'friends', of whom God would
say at the conclusion of the story, "You have not spoken of me
what is right, as my servant Job has" (42:8).

God's treatment of him, Job complains is incredible, unintelligible (v. 12). The "monster of the deep" in pagan myths
was Tiamat, a legendary sea monster which appears in several
ancient writings. Job has never been like the rebellious sea
monster. The Old Testament only uses this language of myth in
poetic contexts, as here.

We have another picture of his physical distress in verses
13-14, where Job is frightened by nightmares, so that he is afraid
even to sleep. Night means no rest for this weary, broken man,
and this seems to be an integral part of God's torment. His
conclusion is that life is not worth living, and he cries to God to
back off, and give him a little respite before the end comes
upon him (v.16). He has no problem with contemplation of the
looming probability of death, what torments him is the slippery
slope by which he will arrive at this final destiny.

What is man that you make so much of him?

This sounds like an intentional parody on Psalm 8, which
celebrates the grandeur of man, made a little lower than the
angels. Job uses the language of the psalm to point to his
ignominy and shame. Why does God even bother with such an

insignificant creature? Why does he torment a wind-blown leaf? Here is his extraordinary conclusion. The very fact that God is always on man's back, always harassing him, always scrutinizing him, is in itself suggestive of the love that God holds towards this being. He is indeed the "Watcher of men" (v.20). Once again we feel the tension in Job's thought between the two faces of God. See Box 6.

Verse 21. Death is inevitable for Job. For some strange reason God has forgotten his normal ways, but when the mood is over, he will come looking for him, to be kind to him again, but it will then be too late, for he will be among the dead. Here is Job's astonishing faith. *"You will search for me..."* In spite of his suffering at God's hands, the crazed and crazy hunter seeking to destroy him, he is convinced that back of it all God still cares for him. His old faith is already beginning to assert itself.

Christian Reflections

7:1: Job's personal sufferings lead him to reflect on the lot of man on the earth – "hard service" is the way he describes it. The Christian would accept that human life is hard, a fulfilment of the condemnation of Adam at the Fall, "by the sweat of your brow you will eat your food" (Gen. 3:19), but would want to stress how this has been modified through Jesus and the Gospel. Christian life is marked by joy (I Pet. 1:8), so that even when Paul and Silas are severely beaten up and thrown into prison, they are found cheerfully singing (Acts 16:22-25).

How far would you say that your own life is "hard service"? How does Christ sweeten this for you? What impedes joy in your life?

7:9: The Old Testament's downgrading of the pagan world's preoccupation with death, points to its upgrading of the NOW, of life in God's world, where the Lord himself declares it all "very good" (Gen. 1:31). The Old Testament is to a considerable extent an earthy book. It is concerned with the life of the believer in the present time, his life on earth. It has little to say about pie in the sky when you die, but a lot to say about steak on the plate while you wait! Paul affirms, "Now is the time of God's favour, now is the day of salvation" (2 Cor. 6:2).

Can we believe in a this-worldly faith today? How would this affect the way you live? How does it relate to the further question of life beyond the grave, brought to resplendent reality by the gospel and resurrection of Jesus, (2 Tim. 1:10; 1 Cor. 15:42-43), yet clearly latent at every level of Old Testament faith (Heb. 11:13-16)?

6. Bildad to the attack – Chapter 8

Bildad is a very different character from Eliphaz. Far from being genteel and instinctively kind, he is confrontational and brutal. He has little concern for finer feelings, or for being sensitive to Job's condition. He identifies totally with Eliphaz' basic picture of God as one who hands out rewards and punishments according as people merit them by their conduct.

If Eliphaz is the advocate of experience as the touchstone of truth, Bildad champions tradition and orthodoxy. Get him out of these spheres and he flounders. His faith is summed up in one sentence: "Ask the former generations" (v.8). We who live today are all johnny-come-latelies, whose highest wisdom is to allow the former generations to instruct us by their accumulated wisdom. To Bildad the chain of tradition stretches back to the beginning of time, and there is no refuting that. We recognise the voice of tradition both within the church and within civil society.

A Vicious Swipe at Job – read 8:2-7
Bildad begins by insulting Job. Not for him Eliphaz' polite, kindly approach. Bildad accuses Job in the first instance of being an old wind-bag, a blabbermouth. As Job has rattled on over the past period, encapsulated in chapters 6 and 7, raising searching questions about God's dealings with himself and with mankind in general, Bildad has steadily got hotter under the collar.

His second accusation is that Job is undermining all that tradition has said about the being of God. By pleading his own innocence, Job has implied that God perverts justice. That Job is guilty is crystal clear from his sufferings. This is an important part of the friends' argument. Justify yourself, plead your own innocence, and you are accusing God of injustice. Which is precisely what Job will go on to do. Shocking! When Abraham looked down on Sodom and understood its impending destruction, he could only exclaim, "Will not the Judge of all the earth do right?" (Gen. 18:25). Job, in contrast, implies that it does not work out like that, the Judge of all the earth does not always appear to do what is right. No wonder Bildad was shocked.

His third accusation is a nasty and cruel jab. Job had appealed to his friends for sympathy (6:14), but he'll get not an ounce from Bildad. He wounds where it hurts Job most, in the heart of a father whose children have died tragically – they got what they deserved, and by implication so has he! The setting of Job's early trials in the context of the constant wining and dining of his children (1:4-5, 13-15), seemed in the first chapter to suggest that Job felt some degree of guilt about their misconduct. So Bildad knew just where to dig his knife into Job's heart with maximum effect.

The remedy of Job's problem is quite simple – reformation of character will again bring God's favour (vv. 6,7). There is a pure and simple logic in Bildad's theology. Sort yourself out, return to a life of purity and virtue, and God will restore your good fortune. Ironically, this is precisely what happened at the end of the story (42:12), but not via the route which Bildad advocated.

The appeal to tradition – read 8:8-10
The source of Bildad's faith is not a personal contact with the living God, but the creed, orthodoxy, tradition. Eliphaz at least had an experience, Bildad has only tradition. The wisdom of past times is considerably superior to our own feeble efforts to

understand God's ways, he argues. Our wisdom is to sit humbly at the feet of the old sages and submit to their instruction as infallibly true.

The sermon: "so perishes the hope of the godless" – read 8:11-19.

Since Bildad will permit of no personal pursuit of truth, his sermon is reduced to a collection of proverbial sayings which enshrine the wisdom of the ancients. Yet these sayings have a touch of poetry about them which is quite fascinating. He uses three delightful illustrations to drive home his point: the papyrus, the spider's web, and "a well-watered plant in the sunshine".

The evil man's (Job's) misfortunes are as logical as the papyrus growing in the marsh, which flourishes only as long as it is rooted in its natural watery environment. Uproot it from this setting and the scorching sun burns it up rapidly. God always and inflexibly uproots the wicked man, like the papyrus. Bildad's ALL here means that there is absolutely no exception in God's just dealings with man, and the wisdom of Job will lie in adjusting his sights in accordance with this wise insight.

True, the godless man has great hopes for the future, but one might just as well trust in a spider's web. The web is fascinating and beautiful to look at, but try trusting your life to it, and its will simply disintegrate (vv.14-15), as do the bad man's dreams. He is like a lovely plant, putting down its roots, well-watered, superbly placed for sunshine. But when torn from its spot, it has no life of its own and quickly withers and dies. In contrast, Bildad implies, the good life flourishes through having its roots in godliness. Since Job's former life has withered and died, he is clearly the godless man being punished for his sins (v.13).

Verses 20-22 apply the sermon. True repentance will bring God's smile once more. *"If he had lived at a later period, Bildad would willingly have burnt Job's body in the hope of saving his soul"* (Ellison). Bildad suggests in verse 20 that there is no smoke without a fire. Though he holds open the door of repentance, he leaves no doubt that he considers Job one of the wicked on whom the well-merited judgments of God have fallen. However, he was more prophetical than he could have imagined. When Job's fortunes were restored, Bildad himself was one of the 'enemies' who were clothed with shame, as he humbly begged Job to offer sacrifices to cleanse his own sin (42:7-9).

Christian Reflections

8:5-7: This is clearly a prosperity doctrine. If Job will but reform his life, God will restore his material fortunes, and indeed greatly multiply them. Compare this with Jesus, who was born among the animals and used their eating trough as his cot; who declared that the birds have nests and the foxes holes, but he himself had nowhere to lay his head, and depended on the hospitality of others. Or compare Paul – "troubles, hardships and distresses ...hard work, sleepless nights and hunger...poor, yet making many rich, having nothing, and yet possessing everything" (2 Cor. 6:4-10).

Do you know of anyone of whom it might be said that they became rich because of the gospel, because of Christian service? Do you know of anyone who became poor(er) because of the same? On the other hand, how does Paul's statement (1 Cor. 9:3-12), that the labourer is worthy of his hire in Christian ministry fit into these considerations?

7. Job reacts to Bildad – Chapters 9–10

It is not entirely correct to say that Job reacts to Bildad. It becomes typical of Job's speeches, that he often ignores what has just been said and goes further back to something someone said earlier. Clearly something has been going through his mind and he feels the necessity to say something in response now. This is his third speech, and profoundly disturbing questions are jostling with each other in his mind, to which he is determined to give voice. He is determined to speak out, to raise daring and dangerous questions, which would only further infuriate his friends.

Shall Job take God to court? read 9:1-20
When Eliphaz had had his ghostly visitation in chapter 4, the
hushed voice exclaimed, "Can a mortal be more righteous than
God?" (4:17). Job now accepts that there is truth in this, and it
troubles him. Since he knows himself to be innocent, he is
conscious that the alternative which is beginning to suggest itself
to him, i.e. to challenge God to a public dispute, is an enormous

---

Box 9 – Putting God in the dock.
At this point Job's thought takes an important step
forward. He has been struggling to understand his
dilemma, and he now feels he has a key – a court case
against God! This is very daring. He visualises a hearing
in which he will be the accuser and God will stand in the
dock. This is the thought in 9:3, 14, 16, whilst in verse 32
he states it boldly: "that we might confront each other in
court."

However, he very quickly realised the impossibility
of achieving anything in such a legal confrontation,
because to do so is like conducting one's own case
confronting the most brilliant legal brains in the land,
clever, witty and astute. Your every word would be made
to contradict everything else you had said. In the end you
would end up with egg on your face, publicly humiliated,
reduced to feeling yourself to be nothing but a worm –
besides paying an enormous legal bill! No! No! No! To
argue with God would be absurd.

Nevertheless, Job suggests the possibility of finding
an arbitrator who would 'lay his hand upon us both', and
thus force God to back off. Sadly, he quickly abandons
such a possibility, since there is no such being (vv.33-
35). Yet the idea will not go away. Later it will provide
the essential key to his personal dilemma – his innocence
and God's apparently unjust treatment of him.

impudence on his part. Nonetheless, he gives free rein to the thought throughout chapter 9.

But he subtly uses Eliphaz' main theological plank in a different way than Eliphaz had intended. Since God is always right and man is always in the wrong, how could anyone dispute with him (9:3)? "He could not answer him one time out of a thousand" means that puny man would be tongue-tied when confronted by God. He would be barraged by a thousand questions, a thousand accusations, a thousand reasons, none of which he could answer. He would be left babbling incoherently.

Such a dispute must be seen against the reality of the immense wisdom and power of God displayed in the vastness of the universe, which Job contemplates in dread (vv.4-10). Such wisdom and power can only leave man floundering in despair. True, Job's God is not easy to live with. He is no tame, loving old grandfather, rather his anger is to be discerned in all parts of his created order (v.5). He is ever at odds with man, and the whole cosmos, and Job is puzzled to understand God's ways (vv.12,13).

How, then, can Job ever hope to get a hearing for his case? The whole thing seems totally unfair. "Who can say to him, 'What are you doing?'" (v.12). You can't call God to account.

Since it is impossible to dispute with God, Job feels himself frustrated. The situation is totally unjust. He has done no wrong, yet he has been made to suffer intolerably. There ought to be some way, somewhere, that he can defend himself. His friends will not give him a hearing. He clings to the idea of a legal dispute with God (v.14), but continues to acknowledge the impossibility of this (vv.14-20). Before the power and shattering anger of God's might (vv.12-13), how totally foolish to think that he could find the necessary words to argue and defend himself (vv. 14-20).

Though Job were to issue his own summons to God to appear in court – surely a daring thought! – he cannot believe that God would give him a hearing (v.16). Instead, "he would crush me with a storm," and only increase his suffering, like an infamous judge who mercilessly increases sentences for the accused for wasting his time by pleading innocent! Job concludes with a desperate statement of the total futility of his situation (v.20). God would so crush him that even his own mouth would be the agent of his condemnation.

I am not guilty! read 9:21-35

The word 'although' has been introduced by the translators in verse 21. The Contemporary English Version, like many other modern translations, read as our title. Job is clearing himself in the light of the impossibility of getting a hearing from God. Of course that is a dangerous procedure, and he recognises that fact, but he is determined to risk everything – "I have no concern for myself, I despise my own life." If God should destroy him for what he is about to say, then so be it. It would actually be a relief from his present suffering.

And what Job says is astonishing. One must imagine the sheer anger, the shaking heads, perhaps even threatening gestures, which his friends now display toward him: "God destroys the innocent along with the guilty!" (v.22).

With one sentence he aims to undermine his friends' carefully constructed creed. They argued tenaciously that God "does not reject a blameless man or strengthen the hands of evildoers" (8:20). Job now argues the contrary, and uses two illustrations taken from human life. When plague sweeps over a population, as frequently happened in past times, it is no respecter of persons. In such occasions the good die like flies, the same as evil people. To use another example, when the legal system of a land falls into the hands of corrupt judges, it is the innocent who suffer, and God seems indifferent. In fact, he argues, one could say that it is God who ordains it that way – "If it is not he, then who is it?" (vv.23-24). Note that Job seems to know nothing of secondary causes, e.g. Satan, though we may have to revise that statement later on, see end of chapter.

This is a flat denial of his friends' view of life. It was dangerous, daring and courageous, but he will risk all. The die is cast! There seems to be no moral order in the universe. The idea is not explored here, but it will return to become the basis of later argument. Disaster falls on all, indiscriminately, and ultimately it lies within the will of God.

Behind these brash words, we must recognise that there is a burning desire in Job's heart to believe that *God is a responsible Being*. It is precisely because reality seems to deny it that his heart cries out in anger against the awfulness of real life. He refuses to live in ivory dream castles, as his friends seem to, and he insists in rubbing their noses into the grimness of reality.

After this violent outburst, in a more subdued mood (vv. 22-24) Job laments the swift flight of his wretched life. He turns from argument to thinking out loud, in a passage marked by reflection, meditation and prayer, which concentrates on his own miserable condition (vv. 25-35). From this point he will often ignore his friends completely and simply let them hear something of the turmoil going on in his own mind. This only serves to infuriate them.

His general point, that all mankind suffer, is exemplified in his own case. He laments his miserable physical condition. He has tried numerous ways to ease his pain, but achieves nothing. It only gets worse. But his physical sufferings pale when confronted with the mental agony of knowing himself condemned at God's bar without a hearing (vv.25-31).

The need of an arbitrator – read verses 32-34.
It is at this point that a new idea forces its way forward in his thinking. Since he cannot hope to argue his own case in court with God, what he needs is an arbitrator, someone who would have the power to make God see sense, and force him "to remove God's rod from me, so that his terror would frighten me no more".

Of course, such a mediator could not possibly be human. No man could put pressure on God. So it must be someone divine. But here lies another problem for Job. His thinking works strictly within the context of monotheism, the belief in one, and only one divine being. "Hear, O Israel, the LORD our God is one LORD." In the pagan world each man, each family, each community, each city, each nation had a personal god who acted as his/its advocate in the council of the gods, who were too busy to give attention to individual cases. Job knows of no other gods. Would that there were! He knows his wish is futile, it is a pipe dream, from which he turns abruptly (v.35). But he has opened up a thought: the possibility of a Mediator to arbitrate his cause in his litigation with God.

Christian Reflections

9:13: "the cohorts of Rahab." This strange expression will puzzle the modern reader. The only Rahab you know is the prostitute on the walls of Jericho, who gave help to the Israelite spies in Joshua 2. But throughout this book, and in several other places in the poetry of the Old Testament, a sinister trio appear – Rahab, Tiamat, and Leviathan (3:8; 41:1-34) – a trinity of evil. They were well-known to the people of Job's world, for they dominated primitive forms of religion. The mention of any one of them would strike terror into the heart of the pagan. Rahab was the female monster of chaos. Yet here in Job the monster, with all her powers, trembles at the feet of Job's God! Hallelujah!

What parallels might we find in the New Testament with this picture of powers of evil threatening us, over which the Lord claims a resounding, paralysing victory? See Colossians 2:13-15, especially verse 15; Hebrews 2:14. The life of Jesus was a titanic conflict with the powers of evil, which Jesus effectively crushed in his death and resurrection.

9:21: "I am blameless." This is a daring affirmation of Job, which shook and angered his friends, and which even some modern Christians may find puzzling. Perhaps you find it easier to identify with the friends than with Job? Never lose sight of the fact that at the end of the story God affirms that Job had spoken well (42:7).

How does this statement sit with the New Testament truth

**that we are all sinners meriting God's condemnation, and
that we are only saved by faith in Jesus?**

9:22: "He destroys both the blameless and the wicked." This is
surely a shocking statement. It infuriated his friends. How do
you react to it? Compare Ecclesiastes 9:2-3, where the skeptic
philosopher argues that evil affects us all indiscriminately. In
contrast consider the words of Jesus, which say the same thing
from a positive angle: God "causes his sun to rise on the evil
and the good, and sends rain on the righteous and the
unrighteous" (Matt. 5:45).

**How far is Job right? How far is he wrong? What modern
events suggest that there is an element of truth in what he
says?**

9.33: "If only there were someone to arbitrate between us."
Conscious of his own inability to confront God, and to seek
justice, Job longs for a go-between to put his case to God. The
Christian will be conscious of the need of a Mediator at a more
profound level, a mediator, not for personal justification, as Job
desired, but for salvation from merited condemnation. There is
no better way to understand the function of Jesus on behalf of
the sinner. The New Testament uses several figures to suggest
this. He is our advocate (I John 2:1-2); our high priest (Heb.
4:14-16); the shepherd and overseer of our souls (I Peter 2:25).

**Have you claimed Jesus Christ as your mediator with
God? Do you know of any other mediator? Do you believe
that Jesus is all-sufficient for you?**

8. "I loathe my very life" – Chapter 10

This chapter is an impassioned prayer to the Almighty. The
cause of the prayer is an intense loathing of his situation. We
must never lose sight of Job sitting on this terrible garbage heap,
scraping his sores with broken pottery. He is utterly sick of life.
9:32-35 had lifted the veil on a brief glimpse of hope for a
mediator to defend his cause, but this was dashed by despair.

He now gives way to pent up feelings.

As in 7:11 Job is conscious, probably as much through the angry facial expressions and gestures of his friends, as through his own inherited beliefs, that the course he had embarked upon, in questioning God's justice, was a very dangerous one. At any moment God might swat this ugly little fly and wipe him out of existence. But he decides that it is better to die and have done with it all, than to continue in this endless misery.

Tell me what charges you have against me (v.2) – read 10:1-7. Job's thoughts now take a new turn. Formerly he had asked his friends to define the charges (6:24), now he asks God to do so. Job feels he could bear his sufferings if he only knew what they were for, what sins he had committed. The use of the word 'charges' shows that he is continuing with the language of the court room. Let God press charges. From his side Job could see nothing which justified his affliction. Could it really be that God simply took pleasure in piling up his distress (v.3)? Could it be that God is capricious by nature, that he simply takes delight in tormenting his servants? This is what Job cannot fathom. What is the root of God's apparently cruel treatment? It is an inconceivable mystery.

Could it be that God is so capricious that he thinks and behaves like a mere man (vv.5-6)? It is not that Job wants to believe this, but he can think of no other alternative. The effect would be to say that God "smiles on the schemes of the wicked" (v.3), that God is soft on criminals. Nevertheless this is a question, not a statement. Job will not accept deep down that it could be true. In the long run God knows very well that Job is not guilty.

The undisputable evidence of God's love – read 10:8-12
Incredibly, in bold and striking contrast to what he has just said, Job clings to the goodness of God. His human logic tells him that this impossible situation is caused by the erratic nature of God's dealings. Yet deep down he cannot believe this. Even as

an embryo in his mother's womb God's grace had favoured him (vv.8-11), and in the whole course of his life divinely inspired good fortune had been his lot (v.12). Although he wrestles to understand God's dealings with him, at heart, deep down, he is conscious of the Lord's great love. It is with this conflict that Job wrestles in his discourses.

Job is desperately trying to resolve a tension. He is God's creature (v.8), yet at present there seems to be something illogical in God's treatment of him. He has been taken by a strange mood. Yet Job clings to the conviction that God is fundamentally GOOD, in spite of present appearances.

Yet God's final objective was to humiliate him – read 10:13-22

All his sufferings were designed from the start, even as God formed him as an embryo. Job charges God with having intentionally concealed his true design, caring for Job with love in life but planning from the beginning to suddenly overwhelm him with disaster in later years. It is clear that all God's past kindness was only designed to make Job's present suffering the more acute.

In verse 16, the lion is to be understood as Job himself, being stalked by God the hunter. Job has risen up, like a lion, in his own defence, yet to do so is extremely dangerous. Like the unscrupulous hunter God is (6:4), so now he will use his awesome power to bring the lion down in disgrace. Again and again God attacks Job on his rubbish dump. His 'anger' never abating. His "forces come against me wave upon wave" (v.17), like military might thrown unceasingly into battle.

Since God designed Job's sufferings from the start, why was he ever born (vv.18-22)? The whole situation is illogical, so that Job reverts to his first agonised cry of pain in chapter 3, longing that he had never been born, or at least that he might now be allowed to die peacefully. Again, it is not death which frightens Job, but the terrible agonies he must face en route.

Job's last fling at the end of this prayer is that he might be allowed a little space of relief in the few days that are left to him. Give me a short respite before I die! It is important here to notice his description of death (vv.21-22). It is decidedly not the "happy land, far far away", as an old song celebrated it, rather it is a place of darkness and gloom. It is left to the gospel of the Lord Jesus to "bring life and immortality to light" (2 Tim. 1:10).

Christian Reflections

Verse 8: "Your hands shaped me and made me." Do you, like Job, picture yourself as God's child? Do you sense and understand the grace of God in his passionate concern for your good? There is a rich faith here, and through all his suffering it is the anchor of Job's soul. But remember that this foundation of his life, this anchor of his soul, was there before his sufferings began.

Do you think he could have weathered the storm if this foundation had not been in place before his sufferings began? What does this say about your own life? Are you prepared for suffering? If it hit you hard, would your faith stand up to it?

Verse 16: "You stalk me like a lion." Some of the things Job says about God may cause us deep concern. This is rough language to use of God's ways. Yet even Jesus asked the great WHY? question on the Cross, as did the psalmist: "Why are you so far from saving me?" (Ps. 22:1).

Do you think that this book enables us to say that it is not wrong to ask "why?" out of the agony of our suffering? How do you react when your world falls apart? Do you sometimes feel like calling God to account?

9. Zophar's Angry Reaction – Chapter 11

We have seen that Eliphaz appealed to religious experience, and Bildad to tradition handed down from earlier generations. Zophar's appeal, however, is to human wisdom, or perhaps better to common sense. For him there are no mysteries. So he finds Job's heart-searching quest for an answer to the mystery of his sufferings totally baffling. He regards Job as a babbler who must at all costs be silenced, and since no one else seems able to do it, Zophar himself will have a go (vv. 2-3). But in so doing he is much more brutal than the others.

What particularly shocked Zophar in Job's speech was his claim to innocence (v. 4). In Zophar'r eyes Job's suffering is in itself an evidence of guilt, a supreme evidence, from which there is no argument. Job shows himself a godless man by pleading his own innocence! The only mystery in Zophar's eyes is that God has not yet answered Job's blasphemies (v.5). In fact, and this must surely be the cruelest jibe of all, "God exacts of you less than your guilt deserves" (verse 6 in Revised Standard Version). In other words, for all his sufferings Job is getting off lightly. This remark is shocking. Job's sufferings are more intense, more dreadful than anything we can imagine, yet this man can say that he is getting off lightly. Zophar, who had suffered nothing, is totally insensitive to Job's anguish.

What incenses Zophar is not only Job's protestations of innocence, but also his burning desire to understand God's ways better. The man of common sense has no time for such mystical quests. Zophar's appeal is to wisdom, the wisdom of men, and he believes that to be identical with God's wisdom.

God's ways are incomprehensible to man – read 11:7-12
It seemed to Zophar that Job was trying to "fathom the mysteries of God", and such a futile quest makes Job into an incredibly stupid man. In reality Zophar is a shallow agnostic. He has never hungered after God, or tried to understand his ways himself, and cannot understand Job's search. In effect he says, Who do

you think you are? God is unknowable. Your desire to understand God's ways better is incredible insolence, if not total
heresy.

What is more, if God were to respond to Job's cry for a court
hearing, the results would be totally disastrous for him, because
God "recognises deceitful men" (vv.10-11). Job may be able to
cover his tracks in the eyes of men, but God's penetrating eyes
discover all evil. Once again we note the absolute conviction of
Zophar that Job must be guilty, for his disastrous state is living
evidence of God's anger (v. 12).

Eliphaz had called him a fool, Bildad called him godless, to
Zophar he is brainless, with no more sense than a donkey. His
awkward questions are a sign of stupidity.

An uplifting sermon of moral clichés – read 11:13-20
Zophar concludes with a sermon built on the "if...then"
structure. Job's future restoration and happiness is conditional
on certain requirements. His friends have these provisos
carefully worked out. It is all quite simple. There is no need to
look for, and attempt to resolve, the mysteries of life. Let Job
"put away the sin that is in your hand," let him yield to God
again in full and glad surrender, and everything will be answered.
It is all so simple to this man of common sense.

These are the conditions. The results are dangled temptingly
before Job's eyes (vv.15-19). Everything will be rosy in his
garden, all his troubles will disappear as a vague, distant
memory. His place in society and his fortunes will be restored.
However, Zophar ends his discourse with a final warning, that
if Job refuses this way of reconciliation with God, then the
consequences will be disastrous (v.20) since God is relentlessly
just and always punishes the wrongdoer.

Christian Reflection

Verse 7: "Can you fathom the mysteries of God?" Zophar's belief that man's search for God is futile, is echoed by many in today's world. We must choose between shallow agnosticism and living faith. There is, of course, an element of truth in it, but not in the sense that Zophar meant it. God reveals to us what we cannot of our own ability discover.

Compare Zophar's words with those of Jesus (Matt. 11:25-30). The "little children" are his disciples, who have come humbly, confessing their ignorance, to receive his teaching. Compare I Corinthians 1:26-31. How do you identify with this?

"Your Maxims are Proverbs of Ashes"
Job's reply to Zophar, Chapters 12–14

Our title catches the spirit of Job's broadside blast against his friends in chapters 12–13. Chapters 12–14 are Job's longest discourse, and it is a very important one. It represents a decisive turning point in the debate, a point at which he takes the initiative and puts his belligerent friends on the defensive. He sets out the bankruptcy of traditional wisdom and theology when faced with an exceptional case like his own. He teaches us that truth cannot be poured into a simplistic mould.

A sarcastic reply to Zophar – read 12:1-3 with 11:12
Job has now heard out all three friends. He has been stung by their unkind, judgmental attitude. What is more, Zophar's words were the unkindest of all. He had boldly stated that Job was a witless man, about as thick as a wild donkey. Job feels derided, jeered at. A smarting Job now turns his full blast on them (vv. 2-3). He first defends himself on the intellectual level, by insisting that he is every bit as intelligent as they are, and in the body of the chapter he will demonstrate this. "Who does not know all these things", means that the teaching they parrot is

old hat, showing no original thought. Notice that in 12:3 and 13:2, at the beginning and end of the passage, we have the same statement, word for word, "I am not inferior to you." This shows how much Job had been stung by Zophar's crude statements accusing him of being stupid, and that it is right for us to interpret this chapter as an endeavour to prove his scholarly abilities.

Job is a special case – read 12:4-6
All the arguments of traditional piety, simply do not fit his case. He had spent years as an example to all, in flawless goodness. He had enjoyed a life of obedience to God, insofar as this was possible, yet he has been reduced to an object of ridicule to everyone.

> *I am a laughing-stock to my friends,*
> *I, who called upon God and he answered me,*
> *a just and blameless man, am a laughing-stock.*

His friends, "men at ease" (v.5), treat him with contempt, calling him a blabber mouth and a brainless donkey. Since they have not had to suffer as he has, this is sure evidence that they are better men than he, in their own eyes.

This causes Job considerable distress, for it highlights a problem which haunts his thinking – that "those who provoke God are secure" (6b), whilst he, the perfect picture of a thoroughly good man, has become an object of contempt.

Job parrots the teachings of the wise – read 12:7–13:2
The bulk of chapter 12 may seem strange to the reader. It appears as though Job is suddenly agreeing with everything his friends have claimed. Take for example the following: "Is not wisdom found among the aged?" (v.12), which reminds us very much of Bildad's arguments in favour of tradition. It is important to understand what Job is doing throughout this passage. He is treating them to a deluge of traditional proverbial sayings, which were taught in the schools of the wise men. He shows his friends

that he is just as knowledgeable in the ancient traditions as they are, so that they have no right to treat him as an ignoramus. There is no need for us to go into these in detail, since Job's point in using them is only to show how limited these maxims are.

13:1-2 ram this home. The repetition of, "I am not inferior to you" (12:3 and 13:2), demonstrates that this is what Job is doing, showing them his equal capacity to recite the lessons learned at school. The whole passage is aggressive and sarcastic. When it comes to learning he is their equal. However, this is just the repetition of abstract, timeless ideas, which avoid the harsh facts of life.

In conclusion he feels that he has proved his case to them, and he now insists that the best they can do is to shut up altogether (v.5).

Job desires a confrontation with God – read 13:3-5
Job presses his idea of a court case with God. "You keep preaching little moral sermons at me. I want to meet God; I want to talk with him; I want to reason with him." It is important to emphasize here that nothing less than a personal encounter with God will suffice for Job. He cannot accept that God is merely the unknowable, as Zophar had argued (11:7). Job rejects Zophar's shallow agnosticism. He wants to know God. His friends will not accompany him on this quest, in fact they have been horrified by the whole idea. Should one confront God he would be annihilated by his holiness and power, much more so to dispute with him.

In contrast with his desire, Job's friends are plasterers of lies (v.4). So far from bringing comfort to a person suffering grave hurt, they are "worthless physicians", and the only wisdom they can show is to stop their jaw-jaw altogether.

The uselessness of trying to defend God – read 13:6-12
Job now demands that they listen to him for a change (v.6). His is not an intellectual discourse, of which he has shown himself

Box 10 – You are all useless doctors. Chapter 13:4
This is Job's description of the speeches of his three friends thus far. In his distress he has shared his agony with them, in the expectancy of finding sympathy and comfort, but finds only opinionated traditionism. In one sense they are pawns of Satan, his third line of attack. Yet in another sense they are God's tools, though by no means in the sense that they thought of themselves as such. They are instruments, designed to so increase his agony, that they drive Job back on God alone!

As physicians, they only irritate the pains they think they are healing. Their ideas are sound in general terms, but totally insensitive to Job himself, and quite wrong in their attempt to apply their rigid creed to him like a straightjacket. They are quite unprepared to rethink anything. As counsellors, they lecture and preach at their counsellee. **True words may be bad medicine for a wounded heart.** Nevertheless, we must allow that they do their best with their doctrinal system.

And herein lies a problem for Job, for they are his old self. Before this terrible experience he would have used all their arguments. He had regarded his own comfortable life as the Lord's reward for his goodness. But that belief has had to go, and he is struggling for something to replace it. Yet he is in danger of coming adrift in an ocean of speculation. Only the Lord can save him from it.

perfectly capable in chapter 12, but a heartfelt plea for a hearing from God. They are shocked by this and wish to defend God against the attacks and complaints of men (vv.7,8), to play God's advocates, his defence counsel. But it is useless to try to defend God's ways before men.

This is a bold, even incredible statement. To play God's advocate is the height of folly (vv.7-8). The temptation to manipulate the facts so that they fit your picture of God is unacceptable. God is as much searching out their integrity as they claim he is for Job. To smear Job with lies is to invite the anger of God. They might deceive men by their show of piety and righteous indignation, but God knows the inner man, and will shortly terrify them (vv.10-11).

Triumphantly, Job feels that he has won the day, concluding that he has reduced his friends' arguments to a heap of rubble:

Your maxims are proverbs of ashes;
Your defences are defences of clay (v.12).

Job prepares to defend his case at God's bar – read 13:13-19
They tried to intervene at this point (13a), but he tells them to pipe down. It is his turn to speak, and he will tolerate no interruptions.

To reason with God may be to risk destruction, he admits, but he is prepared for that, for he has one certainty to cling to: the essential goodness of God. **Though he slay me, yet I will trust him** (v.15). This is the brilliant antithesis of faith. God is the ruthless hunter who is pouring his poisoned arrows into Job, yet he is fundamentally good; he is smashing Job's life to pieces, yet he is worthy of trust. Though God is the originator and executor of Job's troubles, he clings to the belief that God is fundamentally good. As someone has expressed it, he trusts in God, in spite of God.

Again, this stresses the tension between his experience of 'the LORD' through decades past, and the apparent contradiction as he meets God as the Almighty, whose ways are totally puzzling to the human mind. Yet he longs to appear before 'the LORD' or before 'the Almighty', call him what you will, and this very fact strikes Job as strong evidence in favour of his cause, of his innocence (v.16). No godless man can appear, dare appear, before God. Job's very bravado is evidence enough of his godliness (though his friends thought otherwise). What person, who had a stain on his conscience, would hazard an encounter with the all-powerful God?

In fact, Job has now reasoned out his case, the terms of his argument, and he invites his friends to pay careful attention to his reasoning (v.17). He knows what he will argue in court, and above all, *"I know I will be vindicated."* Here is his daring faith. He knows himself innocent, and, therefore, a just God will vindicate him. But there is the problem, this same God is his accuser and tormentor.

Back off, God! – read 13:20-27
Now he turns to prayer and makes two simple requests: (1) Stop punishing me, and don't crush me with terror (v.21, GNB); (2) Issue a writ as plaintiff (v.22), or let me be the accuser. The word 'summons' is distinctly legal terminology, so that Job is here pressing his demand for a court hearing with God. Since God won't answer Job's summons, let him issue his own. Job is willing to present himself in court as defendant. He pleads with God, *"How many wrongs and sins have I committed? Show me my offence and my sin."* Let God spell them out, one by one, and it will be an immense relief for Job to know that there are specific wrongs which he has done, and for which he is being punished. Personally he knows of none. If only there were a reply to this question, his sufferings would be infinitely more tolerable.

We must here imagine a long pause as Job awaits a reply, but he looks vainly to the stony vault of heaven for an answer. This increases his agony. How many a sufferer has likewise lifted his agonised cry to heaven, apparently to be met only by total silence. The heavens are brass, there is no way through to an audience with God. Yet heaven's silence will work in Job's favour, for it suggests there is no charge to be brought!

Job, however, is like a fearless hunter, crashing his way through the jungle of human ideas and emotions, trying to find some safe haven in which to rest secure. His old faith, his old belief in a God who upholds absolute standards of justice, who punishes evil and rewards good, the God of retribution and reward, is in danger of withering away, but so far from being an end to faith, Job is desperately struggling for something new. We now hear him reaching out on a new track.

Why does God persecute a nobody (vv.25-28)? Because that nobody is a somebody in his eyes! Job is conscious of being a weak, fragile human, who, like a leaf, has been blown down, is in the process of dying, and for whom there is no hope. Why does God bother with him? Why should he continue to torment one who is no better than a dead leaf blown hither and thither by the wind (v.25)? Yet this very absurdity holds within itself the promise of a caring God. The logical thing would be for God to simply wipe his hands of man, but instead God continues to deal with him, even if negatively, perhaps even destructively. And in this there is a glimmer of hope.

Yet, pessimism prevails, and Job returns to the court room imagery. God has actually taken to writing down (legal term) charges, without giving him the fairness of showing him the details. He feels that the case against him may go so bad that he is already a condemned man. He will be placed in the stocks, the object of ridicule, as indeed he is already. Like a slave, his feet will be branded, leaving tracks wherever he goes, so that he can never get away from his cruel master.

Chapter 13 concludes with Job passing from himself to man in general, undoubtedly in preparation for chapter 14. In fact, his case highlights man's disaster. What is true of him in particular is true of man in general, he "wastes away like a garment eaten by moths".

Christian Reflections

Verse 3: "I desire...to argue my case with God." This is surely a very bold, his friends would say a very dangerous, desire. Interestingly the same expression is used in Isaiah 1:18, where it is the Lord himself who uses it to offer to sinful men the possibility of being reconciled. Perhaps the idea of seeking reconciliation with his adversary, rather than winning a law suit against him, is what Job himself intends.

Do you think Job was right to desire such an encounter

with God? Would you wish to argue your case with God?
What other recourse do you have? See 2 Corinthians 5:18-21
for the concept of reconciliation.

Verse 8: "Will you argue the case for God?" There is a strong
tendency in some Christians to act as God's advocate. They are
always out to defend his ways, to argue his case, to shut the
mouths of agnostics, atheists and heretics. But it is possible to
win an argument and lose a soul! The apostle Paul renounced
all such attempts, see 2 Corinthains 2:1-4.
   **Are you ever tempted to win an argument for God? Is
this good? What did you achieve? What does Paul see as the
better way (v.2)?**

Verse 15: "Though he slay me, yet will I hope in him." What an
extraordinary statement. At one level we might say that this is
the theme of the whole book. Here is God bent on his destruction,
yet Job clings tenaciously to the idea that in the long run God's
intentions are pure, are for his good.
   **Do you hold such a hope? Have there been any set of
circumstances in your life, or in the life of anyone known to
you, which have caused great distress of thought to you,
about God's dealings with you? Were you/they able to cling
in hope?**

Job charges God *in absentia* – read 14:1-6

Since God will neither present himself in court at Job's demand,
nor summon Job to appear, Job accuses him in his absence.
One can imagine here a court scene in which Job is the accuser,
but he addresses an empty chair, which represents God playing
hooky from Job's court. It is once again a very daring figure of
speech, and must have sent shudders down the spines of his
friends. The accusation is: "Man born of woman is of few days
and full of trouble." Not only is God's treatment of Job himself
unjust, but so is God's treatment of mankind.
   Man's lot is given in two melancholy metaphors. His life is
like the withered flower, and like the fleeting shadow. All his

vanity and pride, all his dreams and accomplishments, all his arts and creative abilities, are summed up here, the sum of his earthly pilgrimage.

Like his own case – the wind-blown leaf which God continually torments – so, astonishingly, God fixes his eyes on every man, searching out the impurities of his life, and setting severe limits on his happiness and security. Job's reaction is the same as he had desired for himself, a request for God to back off and leave man alone (v.6).

The terrible finality of death – read 14:7-12
Here the key word is "hope" (vv.7 and 19). Even a tree is luckier than man, for when you chop it down it will sprout again. You may leave only a stump in the ground, but at the first scent of rain it will spring into new life. Not so man, for whom death is the final doom. The Old Testament presents death as at best a shadowy existence. Indeed, the very word used for movement in the after-life is *rephaim* which means "shadows".

It is this terrible finality of death for man which deeply troubles Job. It is not that he fears death in itself, but that it puts an end to all man's life ambitions, hopes and energies (vv. 10-12). See Box 11 for an explanatory note on death in Job and in the Old Testament as a whole.

A startling hope – read 14:13-17
We must emphasise here that Job is on an adventure of faith's discoveries. His old version of truth has collapsed, like a bridge, behind him, and there is no way of going back to the neat little world of his friends. His props have given way. However, he does not throw in the towel; instead he embarks on a voyage of discovery – searching, seeking, thinking, probing.

Job does not fear death, indeed it would be a wonderful release from his present misery. What appalls him is its terrible finality. For the Christian, life after death is a given truth; not so for Job, and, indeed, Old Testament believers in general. At this point a new thought insists on asserting itself. Job prays that he may enjoy all the benefits of death without its terrible

Box 11 – The horror of death

Death is a major preoccupation for Job. Each of his speeches to this point closes with reflections on the subject. His first instinct had been to desire that he might have died at birth, thus escaping the harsh realities of his present disaster (3:20-22). His next reaction is to be frightened at the sheer brevity of life as it hurtles to its conclusion (7:6). In his third speech, 10:20-22, he desires just a short period of respite from his sufferings before he is confronted with the certainty of death. So far from death being an entrance into a happy home of relief, and a place of untold joy, he views it as "the land of gloom and deep shadow".

Now in chapter 14 he views death more thoughtfully. Man's life on earth is brief and full of trouble. Death ought to be a relief for him, but rather he contemplates it with grim foreboding. It is the inevitability of death and its terribly finality which dismays Job. There is hope for a tree, you cut it down, but its roots send out new shoots. In contrast, for man death is the end (v.12). When he is cut down in death, it is to confront eternal sleep, from which he will never awake. It is not till he resolves his own inner conflict that Job is able to discover the solution to this problem – this terrible finality of death.

finality. Startled, he realises where his thoughts have led him. Something beyond Sheol, the grave! *"If a man die, will he live again?"* He gropes for life after death. If he could be assured of that, his present torment would be bearable (v.14).

Indeed, there will be a day when Job would hear again God's call, so long silent in Job's present agony, and he will joyfully respond. Once again the old harmony with his Creator, which had for so long marked his life would be restored, and God would take no account of any of his defects (vv.15-17).

The momentary hope fades – read 14:18-22

Sadly, Job thrusts this vision from him. Hope is vain. Broken, Job collapses on the dung heap, as he accepts that death, with all its finality, is all he can hope for. The bright dream of verse 13 is dismissed as an illusion. He chooses brilliant images to show that God himself is engaged in smashing man's hope of the after-life – the eroding mountain crumbles to fragments, the rock of hope is torn from its place, torrents remorselessly washing away the soil. Such are the figures of man's hope.

Life on earth continues, but man, who once held such high opinions of himself, knows nothing of it. Strangely, however, the dead man in Sheol does know the decay of his own body. A final touch to the black picture of human misery.

Christian Reflections

Verses 2 and 10: "Man...springs up like a flower and withers away.... Man...breathes his last and is no more." The apostle Peter appealed to verses from Isaiah (40:6-8) to stress this same idea: "All men are like grass, and all their glory is like the flowers of the field; the grass withers and the flowers fall" (I Pet. 1:24). Man in the 21st century has succeeded in adding another ten years to the seventy of Psalm 90:10, for most of us. Perhaps in this new century he will add a few more, but he cannot escape Job's judgment – his days are numbered, he will wither away and perish for ever on earth, and beyond that? Job's confrontation with the perplexity of death, its seeming finality, is echoed elsewhere in the Old Testament – see Psalm 88:10-12, where death is "the land of oblivion". It is important to realise that the New Testament transformed our expectations of life beyond the grave: "Christ Jesus destroyed death and brought life and immortality to light through the gospel" (2 Tim. 1:10).

Consider the brevity of your own life, of the family, relatives, friends, workmates, neighbours, who surround you. What hope do they have beyond the brief years of their earthly lot? What hope do you have?

11. Eliphaz to the Attack – Chapter 15

In this chapter Eliphaz, Bildad and Zophar begin their second round of speeches, led by the first named. They will cling stubbornly to their rigid positions, repeating constantly their clichés about the dreadful destiny that always falls on the wicked. This rubs salt into Job's wounds since he knows they see him as the prime example of the wicked man being punished by a righteous God.

We have seen Eliphaz before (chs. 4–5) as a polite, softly-spoken man, trying to reason with Job. In this chapter we see him with a different tone of voice. There he had spoken in the role of a wise man, restraining his temper, holding himself in check, seeking to use the mildest language. But as the argument has developed, he has begun to smoulder internally.

You old windbag – read 15:2-6

Eliphaz understood Job's arguments perfectly well, and for that reason was frightened by them. He affirms that Job has rejected all the results of the wise men's studies, and has thus renounced all possibility of being classed among them (vv.2f). Job has attacked the representatives of Wisdom. He is guilty of abandoning the assured conclusions of the Wise. His fierce attack on Zophar's speech (12:1–13:2) has proved this beyond a doubt, and Job's own speech can only be regarded as a belly-full of the hot east wind, the famous and infamous sirocco. Eliphaz reduces Job's heartfelt searching after God to *empty notions.* For Eliphaz this is the only way to treat Job's speeches – with scorn, rather than listen carefully and reply intelligently.

In reality Eliphaz is a frightened man. The apparently solid foundations of his faith are being challenged by this savage who is intent on destroying everything in his path. Moffatt translates verse 4 in this way: "You are doing away with religion." Eliphaz feels threatened. The bedrock of his piety is being undermined. He now knows that Job is a thoroughly evil man (v.5). He has been scandalised by Job's affirmations. The very fact that he speaks as he does is proof-positive of his sin (v. 6).

Who do you think you are? – read 15:7-13
This is a direct confrontation between these defenders of traditional wisdom and the upstart Job. Do you claim a monopoly on wisdom? Wisdom, tradition and theology are all on our side (v.10).

"God's consolations" (v.11) are the advice of his friends. They really did believe that they were offering him the very best advice, and that they had figured God correctly in all they said. We must not judge them too harshly, since they were sincere in believing they were consoling Job. Note the vivid touch in verse 12. In a written account we miss the flashing eyes, the shaking heads, and the attempts to squelch replies. Their opinions of Job's reactions to their "consolations", however, are that he is raging against God, with a torrent of hate pouring out of his mouth.

Eliphaz returns to his basic theme, with an appropriate sermon – read 15:14-35
In his first speech he had spelt out his basic argument: "Can a mortal be more righteous then God? Can a man be more pure than his Maker?" (4:17). This rhetorical question expects an emphatic "No". Eliphaz repeats the creed here, with the implication that since man, every man, including Job, "is vile and corrupt", the only viable solution to his problem is for Job to grovel before God in broken humiliation and confession of his guilt. It is important to realise that for Eliphaz and his friends the subject implied by his rhetorical question is not one of sin and righteousness, needing grace and forgiveness, but of man's vast inferiority before God the omnipotent Creator. The distinction is important. It is best understood in Bildad's conclusion that man is a maggot and a worm (25:6).

Verses 17-35 then give us the content of his sermon, beginning with an exhortation to give careful heed to what he is about to say. Evidently he feels he has something of importance to add, especially since he is giving a distillation of the very best wisdom received by tradition, validated by personal observation. The basic point of his long sermon is, "All his days the wicked man suffers torment" (v.20). This is a step forward in the argument of the friends. To this point they have argued that evil men are always punished by God for everyone to see, now he argues that, whatever their outward condition, inside they are tormented by fear. This is a fairly regular argument used by religious people, and as usual has a grain of truth in it, yet is by no means universally true. Part of the agony of Asaph in Psalm 73 was that so far from being tormented by a guilty conscience, the hearts of the evil rich are calloused, i.e. they feel no remorse whatsoever.

Perhaps both Eliphaz and Asaph are right to a point. There are bad men (and women, though these do not appear in the argument) who are racked by mental torment, but equally there are those who are untouched by any sense of guilt. Both Eliphaz and Asaph yield to a common temptation, to universalise what is partially true, and thus to devalue the truth.

We do not need to go into the details of the sermon, since it is highly repetitive and adds nothing to the argument further than what we have noted here.

Christian Perspectives

Verse 4: "You even undermine piety." Eliphaz feels threatened by Job's refusal to parrot the old ideas, and his attempt to strike out to a newer understanding of God's ways. This is a very natural instinct. The religious leaders felt the same way about Jesus (Mark 2:15-16; 3:16; 7:1-5; 8:31).

How do you handle a believer who seems to introduce new ideas into your circle, your church, your fellowship? Do you feel threatened? Do you panic? Or do you try to listen carefully to what he/she is saying? Might they have something to contribute, some new angle on the truth? What is your measuring stick for truth?

Verse 14: "What is man...that he could be righteous?" Eliphaz' question seems to echo the very heart of the gospel! It is the centre of all his thinking. Job even agrees with him in the general sense (9:2). But somehow his use of it went wrong. At the end God indicates that he has been basically wrong in his argument with Job, see 42:7. Clearly it is possible to embezzle the truth and misapply it! How can this be so?

Is it possible to use the truth untruthfully? Is it possible to misapply it? Is it possible to use it as a club to batter someone, in situations which don't apply? This is obviously a profound question.

12. God has gone Berserk! – Chapters 16–17

Miserable comforters – read 16:1-5
So far from being consoled by Eliphaz' sermon, Job is infuriated. Eliphaz not only makes "fine speeches", he constantly shakes his head while Job is speaking, indicating his exasperation with Job's stupidity. Job, in response, brands his friends, "miserable comforters" (v.2). "God's consolations", offered by Eliphaz (15:11), had been like a knife in Job's ribs, vastly increasing his distress. If the roles had been reversed, Job would have ministered relief to them in their suffering (vv. 4-5). Long-winded, high-minded speeches are of no use to a person in distress.

God is a crazed, savage animal – read 16:6-14
Job turns from useless argument to reflection. He is in a no-win situation (v.6), relentless pain is his lot, and God is the author of it all. His home life is devastated, and his appearance is haggard and gaunt (v.8).

In one of the most incredible statements of the book, he accuses God of behaving like a wild animal, which throws its miserable victim to the ground, gnashing its teeth, bending every sinew in its body in order to destroy its prey. True, it is men who brutalise him (v.10). They slap, punch, and spit in his face

Box 12 – Three clear certainties emerge.

For Job, three clear points are developing in his pursuit for truth:

1. The conventional account of God's governing of the world is fatally defective (chs. 12–14).
2. He is not guilty of anything which would merit the suffering he has been forced to endure (6:12,29ff; 9:15,20ff; 10:7; 12:4; 16:17; 23:12; 27:1-6).
3. He is developing the conviction that somehow, somewhere, somewhen, a just God will vindicate him (16:19-21; 19:23-27).

It is very important at this stage to note these emerging certainties. Whilst for his friends the ground seems to be sinking beneath them, for Job these realities are like rocks on which he can place his feet.

(17:6), but behind them stands God, who has given him up to them (v.11).

In the midst of a supremely happy life, for no known reason, God had shattered him, seized him by the neck and crushed him, made him the target of his enmity. Men are no more than God's archers, who mercilessly *"pierces my kidneys and spills my gall on the ground"* (v.13). Relentlessly, untiringly, God is destroying Job: *"Again and again he bursts upon me; he rushes at me like a warrior"* (v.14). The poor wind-blown leaf has become the centre of God's reckless fury. Are Job's words brash, foolish? He had clearly given careful thought to what he is now saying (v.6).

I suspect that at this point many readers begin to identify more with Job's friends than with Job. His words, his accusations against God, seem virtually blasphemous. But before we condemn him, read God's final verdict on the whole matter in

42:7-9, where the three friends are ordered to ask Job to offer sacrifices to erase their sins, because only Job has spoken well of God in the debate! Perhaps we find that mind-boggling, but we must accept it as God's word to us. We cannot isolate any passage of scripture from the total context of the book in which it is found. So here, we must accept God's final verdict. Be warned, lest God ask Job to purge your folly as well!

Job's only response: deep humility – read 16:15-17
Job's only response to God's brutal frenzy has been marked by desolate mourning, tears of sorrow, humility. His face is swollen and blurred by excessive weeping, his eyes ringed by the impact of sleepless nights. Yet he has maintained his integrity and prayer, in spite of God's brutality. Reduced to utter misery, he has never responded in kind.

There must be justice – read 16:18-21
Deep down, continually breaking through, lies the conviction that God is just, that there must be justice somewhere. Job never wavers from the certainty that he faces certain death, but in that case he is aghast at the thought that he may die without justice having been done, without having been vindicated in the sight of his friends and before the community which has rejected him.

Since man and God alike are deaf to his pleas, Job turns to the earth itself for comfort, for vindication: *"Oh earth, do not cover my blood"* (v.18). He will die very soon, but without vindication of his cause it will be an unjust death. His blood ought to lie on the face of the earth uncovered, appealing to God and man as a perpetual cry for justice. It would be a crime against justice if he dies unheard, his case simply forgotten, swept under time's carpet. Though death stares him in the face, he dares to believe that vindication will come.

So profound is this growing certainty that justice must be done, that a new idea, lurking in the background of his mind, breaks through into consciousness. He dimly detects a figure before God who will vindicate his cause (v.19). Excitedly, he piles on words to describe this dim figure – my witness, my advocate, my intercessor, my friend. He is One who will plead the righteousness of Job's cause in the very presence of God, "in heaven". Who can that be?

Here is the crux of his problem: who can represent him before God? Eliphaz (see 5:1) had denied him the possibility of anyone representing him. Job is gate-crashing his way to a denial of Eliphaz' position. As we have already observed in his second discourse (ch. 9), he had cried, *"If only there were someone to arbitrate between us..."* But no such being was available, since Job, as universally in the Old Testament, cannot believe in any other divine being but the one true God. Other religions in his world would have offered him numerous gods to choose from, who could advocate his cause before God. We seem to hear an echo of that in the way in which Roman Catholics and others today pray to the Virgin, or to their favourite saint, to advocate their cause with a remote Almighty. No such way was open to Job. Who then is his friend in heaven? The answer is not long in coming.

Christian Perspectives

Verses 4-5: Job rebukes his friends for the way they have counselled him in his distress. If their roles had been reversed he would have spoken words of comfort to them. The mentality of the friends was more like that of the people who brought the woman caught in adultery to Jesus (John 8:1-11). How did Jesus treat her?

How would you have counselled Job? How do you counsel sufferers today? How would you converse with a practising homosexual?

Verses 9-10: The reality which Job experiences is the brutality of men (v.10), but behind it he recognizes the brutality of the God who permits them (v.9). This is a frightening concept, but it is also akin to Ephesians 6:12, where our conflict with men is really a conflict with forces of evil which egg them on. Of the brutal death of Jesus, Paul states boldly, that God "did not spare his only Son, but gave him up" (Rom. 8:32). Isaiah 53:10 boldly affirms that "it was the LORD's will to crush him and cause him to suffer". The same could be said of Job's sufferings, and perhaps here we might see his sufferings as a pale shadow of Jesus.

What of your experience of suffering? In the short-term it may be something very, very painful, but in the long run will you be able to say with Paul, "We know that in all things God works for the good of those who love him" (Rom. 8:28)?

Verse 18: "O earth, do not cover my blood." 'Blood' in Scripture means a violent death. The violent death of three men are singled out for mention in the Bible, the blood of Abel, of Jesus, and of Job. The blood of Abel cried for vengeance against his murderer (Gen. 4:10-12). The blood of Jesus "speaks a better word than the blood of Abel" (Heb. 12:24), since it cries for mercy and forgiveness. The blood of Job lies between these two, since it cries for vindication.

How do you identify with each one of these violent deaths, of Abel, Job and Jesus?

Emotion cracks again – read 16:22–17:5

Once again we hear the cry of pain mingled with the expression of hope. Death is a certainty. He may hang out a short time more in this ghastly condition, but only *"the grave awaits me"*, and his journey to that place must be made, accompanied not by the mourning of friends but by the coarse laughter of mockers (17:2).

Yet such a state of affairs cannot go unsolved. There must be justice for Job. But who will vindicate his cause? And here his answer causes us astonishment (17:3):

Give me, O God, the pledge you demand,
Who else will put up security for me? (NIV)

You be my Surety with yourself
for who else can pledge himself for me? (New English Bible)

Box 13 – Development of the Mediator theme, ch. 16.
It is essential here to trace again the court room drama
with which Job confronts his dilemma. He is convinced
of his own innocence, and of the injustice of his friends'
innuendoes. In chapters 9 and 10 he had contemplated
the possibility of a court case with God, but had dismissed
this as absurd, since one would simply find oneself
annihilated by God's superior wisdom and power.

Nevertheless, he suggests the possibility of finding an
arbitrator who would 'lay his hand upon us both', and
thus force God to back off. He quickly abandons such a
possibility, since there is no such being (9:33-35). Yet he
has made a very important step forward and this idea will
not go away and will eventually provide the essential key
to his personal dilemma – his own innocence and God's
apparently unjust treatment of him.

Even now he gropes after the key. His case must be
heard (v.18), and he is persuaded that there is one in God's
presence who will be his witness, his advocate, his
intercessor, his friend (19-21), and dimly he perceives
that this one must in some way be God himself (17:3).

You must go bail for me to yourself. (Jerusalem Bible)

Lay down a pledge for me with yourself,
who is there that will be my guarantor. (New American Standard
Bible)

Be pleased, now, to be responsible for me to yourself;
for there is no other who will put his hand in mine. (Basic English
Version)

You must defend my innocence, O God,
since no one else will stand up for me. (New Living Translation)

Translators wrestle to provide an adequate sense for these difficult words, but what all these are groping after is a way of expressing what Job is trying to say. Perhaps he himself did not yet fully comprehend it, but he feels that in some way his only hope is that God himself will present his case in God's own tribunal. He believes that God himself is to become surety for him, that his cause will be vindicated with God. He gropes after something he barely comprehends.

What is so impressive about Job is that he neither denies God's existence, nor does he look for some other god, some other religion. Though God treats him as an enemy, Job does not turn away from him. Rather he calls on the very God who is crushing him. His only place of refuge is in the very God whom he accuses of brutalising him. He puts his confidence in the One who has reduced him to despair. He claims "as his Defender the One who judges him, as his Liberator the One who throws him in prison, and as his Friend his mortal enemy" (R. de Pury).

His fluctuating emotions employ two sentiments which are prominent in the Psalms: the complaint, and the confession of trust. A large number of psalms, e.g. 22 and 38, express the deep agony of the sufferer. His complaint is an integral part of his distress. It is the scream of despair. It is helpful to reflect that, whatever may have been their origin, these painful psalms were included in the song book of the people, giving voice to their united distress. Those were not easy days.

In many psalms of complaint the psalmist is able to break through to a place, usually based on past experience of God's goodness, where he can declare his conviction that God will bring him out of his suffering to a place of peace and joy. It is a trust in God, in spite of God. It is a trust in God apparently against the odds. In an earlier speech Job had cried, "Though he kill me, I will trust in him." Job is convinced that there must be someone who will take his part against what seems to be God's final ruling. But there is only one who can – God himself. He pits the God whom he has known through a life of blessing against the God he now experiences in grief and shame.

Box 14 – Job's violently fluctuating emotions

The reader may often be puzzled by Job's fluctuating emotions. One moment he is plunged into despair, which leaves us convinced he cannot plumb the depths any deeper; the next he is expressing convictions of hope. In chapter 16 we sense a state of near collapse, in which he portrays God as merciless, as a wild animal set to destroy him, yet by the end of the chapter he is speaking of God as his friend.

We need not be surprised by this. We can so easily forget the very real physical, mental and social catastrophe in which our hero finds himself, and which never leaves him, day or night. We can be so swept up into the argument of Job and his friends that we subconsciously think we are in a comfortable debating chamber.

We must constantly sit with Job on the dung heap. Only there can we understand why his emotions fluctuate so violently. We shall then be amazed that he has any hope at all, why he doesn't just give it up, curse God and die, as his wife had suggested.

We can do no better here than note the words of Hanson: *"Within these limits Job's thoughts wander; now he accuses God of injustice, now he asserts his belief that God would justify him, now he protests that God has refused him judgement, now he says that he will never abandon his plea. The argument in the book does not proceed by logical steps from point to point."*

If we take into account God's final verdict on Job - that he spoke well of God (42:7), we can learn that God even accepts rash words from a sufferer, if only he will cling to God in the inferno of his anguish.

'Friends' and foes? – read 17:4-10

Again notice his unstable emotions. He has just asserted that God is on his side, but now he piles on allegations about the way God is using his friends and his foes to antagonize him even more. For the present he has only the "consolations" of his friends, and these add to Job's despair. He sees in them another of God's chosen instruments of torture. He has closed their minds (vv.4-5), so that they are not even able to listen to Job's arguments. Their speeches goad him, needle him, harass him more and more.

We feel in these verses the pathos of Job's sufferings. He has become a warning to the whole world. As he sits on the rubbish dump, people show their hatred of him by spitting in his gaunt face. He is skin and bones, a shadow of his former noble self. Obviously there were some in Job's society before his fall who envied his success, his wealth, his high position, and who now gloated at his fall. They gleefully tell stories about him (v.6), and when obliged to go out to the rubbish dump, take the opportunity to spit in his face. This deeply humiliated him. It would seem that his only form of sustenance was to scrabble around among the rubbish to find a few chunks of stale bread and rotting vegetables thrown out by the town-dwellers.

He has wept till he has almost grown blind (v.7), and his body has become a scarecrow of his original noble condition. Those with a little more civil consciousness are appalled at the way he is agonising, yet they do nothing about it, though it becomes a cause of contention among the townsfolk (vv.8-9).

He taunts his friends, throwing down the gauntlet to them to show a crumb of intelligence (v.10). He charges them with ignorance, not wisdom, a remark which stung poor Bildad (18:3).

In the depths of despair – read 17:11-16

Verses 11-16 show a man whose every dream, every hope, has come to a crashing end. He stares hopelessly into the jaws of death, knowing that this is the only 'home" he will ever again

inhabit, but at least it will be a place of final rest from the torment
of his suffering. He feels himself virtually fondling the very
worms which will eat up his flesh in the grave. Death in fact
hangs like a grim spectre over this whole speech (16:18; 16:22–
17:2; 17:11-16).

Christian Reflection

Verse 6: "A man in whose face people spit!" Here is utter
rejection by his community. He had once stood high among his
people (ch. 29), a man deeply respected by all. Now people
who have occasion to go to the rubbish heap spit in his face!
What utter loneliness! To suffer is bad enough, but when those
who once respected and supposedly loved you, reject you, this
is agony indeed. Yet out of it Job was to learn many lessons.

**Don't waste your suffering! Have you suffered rejection?
Have family, or friends, or neighbours, or work mates, or
non-Christians, turned against you? Find in the Lord, as
Job was beginning to perceive, your comfort, your strength,
your joy.**

13. The fate of Mr. Badman – chapter 18

Facing the fury of Bildad – read 18:1-4
Bildad is infuriated by Job's speech. He rejects Job's intense
search for God as hypocritical sham. It is clearly quite impossible
to reason with him as the friends were trying to do. Two things
had stung Bildad. First, the accusation that God had closed their
minds to understanding and not a wise man was to be found
among them (vv. 4 and 10).

Secondly, that God is the unjust author of Job's sufferings.
Job had pictured God as a wild animal (16:9), savagely tearing
him to pieces. Bildad assures Job that it is he who is tearing
himself to pieces. For Bildad all Job's speeches are evidence of
a very bitter man, lunging out in accusations against God, against

his true friends, and against society in general. Job has made the world revolve around himself (v.4b). He is to be despised rather than pitied, since he will not take the sensible road of repentance.

The lamp of the wicked is snuffed out – read 18:5-21

Bildad treats Job to yet another pious sermon on the fate of Mr. Badman: The wicked are *always* punished. Since the sermon is a repetition of all that the friends have been saying, and adds nothing new, there is no need to analyse it. Its main theme is indicated in our title, and the content is simply a multiplicity of showy examples of the supposed eternal principle, climaxing with the pontifical statement in verse 21 that Mr. Badman always gets it in the neck sooner or later, and, since God is just, sooner rather than later. Job is, of course, the living example of this principle.

Again Bildad shows himself totally unable to follow Job's anguished questionings. They are simply not on the same wave-length.

Christian Reflections

Verse 17: "The memory of him perishes from the earth..." Bildad's devastating picture of the disastrous fate of Mr Badman is the most comprehensive in the book. He is utterly convinced that every bad person is totally destroyed sooner or later. Is he right? Asaph certainly disagreed with him (Ps. 73), and Job will energetically refute him (Job 21).

What is your own experience in this respect? Are bad people always visually punished for their evil? How do we explain a God of justice if they are not? Think of the rich man and Lazarus in Luke 16:19-26. What does Jesus' parable teach us?

14. "I've been Wronged" – Chapter 19

Chapter 19 is the shortest of Job's speeches, but it is in many ways the most important. Verses 1-22 are a bitter cry against the gross injustice of his situation; whilst verses 23-27 are the glorious climax of his quest for justice. Once again we note that Job's emotions fluctuate within a very short space.

The cruelty of words – read 19:1-7
There is cruelty in the speeches of the "friends", especially in this last one of Bildad. In his reply Job rejects them. All their attempts to instruct him in the way of "truth" only serve to aggravate his sufferings. He is tormented and crushed by their crude attempts to console him. What is worse they use his sufferings to magnify their own supposed virtue, lecturing him with a superior air of self-righteousness, and, instead of expressing sympathy with his sufferings, use them to beat him with (v.5).

God has wronged me! (v.6). Job now states the question at issue with his friends in the bluntest terms. God has unjustly made him suffer, he has stopped at nothing to destroy him. Job's pitiful cry for justice and relief from his agony meets only with a stony silence from heaven (v.7). It takes little imagination to picture the reaction of his friends to this. They will have been shocked to the core by his audacity, by his gall, by his heresy.

Job has been crying to God for justice, for a voice from heaven to explain his sufferings, to either show him the charges against him, or to justify him before his society and before his friends, but the heavens are brass (v.7). In sum, "I've been wronged. There is no justice." His pathetic, helpless cries for fair treatment go unheeded. We might here note the reaction of a French Christian commentator, Terrien: "He the infinite dwarf, the son of clay, the ephemeral moth, has lost the sense of dependence upon God. Job denounces and rebukes his Creator. Man condemns God." I suspect that many of us by this time are beginning to get angry with Job. Let us beware of judging Job harshly. God didn't! (42:7).

God the unscrupulous enemy – read 19:8-12
Job uses a series of graphic word pictures to describe what God has done to him.

> Like a giant he has blocked Job's path,
> He has enveloped his path in darkness so that he can only
>   grope in thick gloom,
> He has defrocked him of his honour,
> He has pulled the bricks out of the building of his life,
> He has uprooted him like a useless tree,
> He burns with anger against him, and, most absurd of all,
> He brings his warriors like an army to lay siege to Job's
>   fragile tent!

This last picture is worth noting. There is absurdity in God's actions. He throws up his siege ramps, brings in his battering rams, as though attacking a heavily fortified walled city, but Job is only a puny *tent*. In these illustrations Job expressed his great perplexity – given his total insignificance, why should God waste his energies on him? Why should God torment a wind-blown leaf? It doesn't make sense to waste his energy on something insignificant. But then, perhaps that is an indication that this insignificant "something" is really of supreme importance to God!

A lonely, deserted man – read 19:13-20
In this paragraph Job turns to another area in which he feels keen distress – his total rejection by his society. He sits on the refuse heap outside the town, the community's reject. We must read chapter 29 in order to catch the pathos of this passage. There he describes in detail the very honourable position he had held in the community. When he appeared in public, "the young men saw me and stepped aside and the old men rose to their feet" (29:8). Now, "Even the little boys scorn me; when I appear, they ridicule me" (v.18).
Everyone has deserted him: brothers, acquaintances,

kinsmen, friends, guests, servants, wife. He has become the object of ridicule among those who once revered his very shadow. *"All my intimate friends detest me; those I love have turned against me"* (v.19).

Only Job's life is left, and that barely (v.20). He sits haggard on the rubbish heap, reduced to skin and bones, a poor, lonely, deserted man, in the pits of despair, with never a moment of relief, day or night, from his unending torment. Yet he knows that God could in a moment relieve him of it all. He does not, and for that reason alone Job knows that God wills his suffering.

An impassioned plea for pity – read 19:21-22

Job turns sobbing to his friends, seeking for a little sympathy and understanding. In all his speeches, and even at the beginning of this one (19:1-5), he had poured scorn on them, but now in his misery he turns to them, choking with tears, for a little human pity. But he will receive not an ounce of sympathy, for in their eyes he is a justly condemned man, whose every word only widens the gap between him and them. Also, God has closed their minds, for they are part of God's weaponry, designed to increase his agony, and so drive him back on God alone as his refuge.

Between verses 22 and 23 we must imagine a long pause. He turns in his agony away from his friends, to heaven itself, but is rewarded with total silence. How long does the silence last? We do not know. Perhaps the encounter with his friends breaks off at this point, perhaps even for days, months. What we do know is that what Job next says is, from his personal point of view, the most significant in the book to this point, and perhaps in the whole.

Faith explodes into flower – read 19:23-27

As often happens, out of his moment of deepest despair Job rises to new faith as he tries to grapple with the meaning of his suffering. He is conscious that he is about to say something of momentous importance. His words should be recorded for future generations. The trouble with the spoken word is that it vanishes into air, unless it is conserved in writing. Job envisages the use of the two methods of ancient conservation in writing, the scroll, and engraving (19:23-24). He first considers the papyrus scroll, but the trouble with this was that it lasted for a very short time, as dampness would rot it quickly. Even engraving on lead would not suffice, since metal would rust and disintegrate over the centuries. No, he must have something that would last into the distant future.

So he turns to the most endurable form – to engrave on rock. Ancient history gives us numerous examples of this, from the pictographic rock art of the cave dwellers, to the hieroglyphics of the Egyptians, to the cuneiform engravings on a towering rock face of Darius the Great at Behistun, Iran. They are still with us. So Job wants what he is about to say "engraved in rock for ever". And what mind-blowing words they are!

"I know that my Redeemer lives!"

To these words we bring minds charged with Christian overtones. But it is probable that Job did not mean quite what we think of his words. It is an excellent example of our tendency to read biblical statements out of context. What did Job intend? Unfortunately this is not easy to determine, principally because the passage is plagued with difficulties of translation (see footnotes in most Bibles). However, though the words may not have the full meaning Christian piety offers, we can at least note the basic sense of Job's intense thought.

Earlier he had verbalised the need for a *mediator* between himself and God (9:33), and had formulated the growing conviction that only God himself could undertake such a role (17:3). Now he names God as his *go'el,* a Hebrew social and legal term in the Old Testament for a near relative who is duty bound to take up one's cause. Sometimes it is translated "relative". The verbal form is found in Exodus 6:6, where God affirms, "I will free you from being slaves...and will redeem you with an outstretched arm." Job has lost his social solidarity, but has found, as suffering Israel had, a true kinsman. The Lord is said to be the *go'el* of the fatherless and the widow (Prov. 23:11). Thus the *go'el* is a near relative who avenged wrongs. Job claims vindication as a right from his God, "my *go'el*". This is the one Job has already named as his 'witness, advocate, intercessor and friend" (16:19-20).

Though the passage has many difficulties of translation, perhaps the sense is best captured in a modern translation:

> In my heart I know that my Vindicator lives
> and that he will rise last to speak in court;
> and I shall discern my witness standing at my side
> and see my defending counsel, even God Himself,
> whom I shall see with my own eyes, I myself and no other
> (New English Bible).

It would be better to translate *vindicator* here. Job knew now that only God could vindicate his cause, not *a god* in the pagan tradition, but the only God, the same one who had himself inflicted Job's life with all this damage. It is not that he returns blithely to the good God he had known for so many years, but that, though "the almighty" God treats him as an enemy, through the blackness and the hell Job does not falter, nor seek another court, but calls upon this same God who apparently takes a peculiar delight in crushing him. He runs to the arms of the very God whom he accuses of causing him so much damage. Surely this is stupendous faith!

But his words take us an important step further. It is difficult to say with confidence that Job is here expressing the certainty of resurrection, though Christians have seen it pointing that way. Not for a moment did he expect the happy ending which we read about in the epilogue. We have seen that each of his speeches to this point end in a contemplation of the certainty of death, which will, physically speaking, be an enormous relief.

Yet a death in which he is not vindicated would be a terrible injustice. Hence his pathetic cry in 16:18: "O earth, do not cover my blood; may my cry [for justice] never be laid to rest." What he sees now is a vindication the other side of death, in which he will personally participate. Three times he stresses that he expects to see his vindication after death with his own eyes. He sees enduring conscious fellowship with God after death. It is as though he experiences a momentary brilliant ray of light from "the other side".

He will say nothing more on this subject, yet as far as the book is concerned, this was the climax of his personal search. This was the turning point. Though he never quite rises to the same point again, the tension has been relieved. He could think more clearly and could set his suffering in a wider framework.

The contemplation of this fills him with indescribable joy as he concludes in verse 27: "My heart faints within me" (RSV).

Job on the offensive (vv.28-29). He concludes by saying in effect, "You, my friends, have put yourselves in a very dangerous position!" He pictures them hounding him, like a pack of baying dogs, since they consider that the root of all his problems lies within himself, not in God, or in circumstances, or in others. Job's own vindication will inevitably mean condemnation for them. Let them beware.

Christian Reflections

Verse 5: "If indeed you would exalt yourselves above me." His friends' attacks not only wound Job's spirit, by implication they are a self-justification. If Job is being punished for his sins, and punished so horrifically, then they must be very much 'good'er men than he, otherwise they would be suffering like he is. As we read the strong language of chapter 16, and again in this chapter, we shall, perhaps, be tempted to side with his friends in condemning him, but in so doing we set ourselves up as better people than he.

Is there any situation in which we might conclude that a suffering person is being punished by God? Does such a

Box 15 – The Living Redeemer.

These verses, 19:25-27, are the crescendo to Job's thoughts about his personal distress. He himself wanted them recorded indelibly for all to read (vv. 23, 24). We have watched his dilemma develop, as he contemplated taking God to court, but dismissed the idea, since he could hardly conduct his own case against the Almighty.

This drove him to contemplate the possibility of finding a mediator who would be able to arbitrate his case with God, but where was he to find such a being? Then we saw that he mused tentatively on the idea that God himself might be his go-between with God. A daring thought!

Now he boldly lays hold on that idea. God himself will be his advocate (verse 25). In Hebrew the word translated 'Redeemer' in our text, carries with it the idea of a near relative who is responsible to care for those of his family who might be in trouble. Job dares to claim his right to appeal to God, with whom he has talked in close harmony for so many decades.

When and where God will vindicate him, he is not sure. But that he himself will be present he has no doubt. A vindication in which he did not personally share would be a shallow victory. But since he is sure that death is staring him in the face, he contemplates vindication beyond the grave, in which he himself will consciously share. Here is the solution both to his questioning of the justice of God and of his horror of the death which most certainly awaits him.

He has no hope of vindication in this life, but now he knew God would vindicate him. "*But (and here is the lamp of faith), a vindication in which he did not share would be a hollow mockery.... He sees continued conscious communion with God after death*" (Ellison). This may not be the full Christian vision of resurrection, but it is very near to it, and paves the way for it.

**conclusion imply that you are better than they? Read Luke
13:1-5. How might the words of Jesus relate to these words
of Job? How might they clarify our thoughts here?**

Verse 7: "I've been wronged!...there is no justice." These bold
words lie at the heart of Job's agony. It is one thing to suffer, it
is another to suffer in a situation in which you can discover no
logical reason why you should be required to suffer. If God is in
control, why does he permit you to suffer so terribly? Has he
abdicated the throne of justice? There is no easy response to
this question. We recognise from multiple New Testament
scriptures that suffering is a tool in God's hand to mould our
characters (Rom. 5:3-5; I Pet. 1:6; James 1:2-4). But it is possible
that by now Job, and those who like him suffer terrible destitution
today, will have learned such lessons as needed to be learned.
What then? We can only find the ultimate solution to the riddle
as we stand, or better kneel, at the foot of the Cross and accept
that God himself has plumbed the depth of our suffering, and
has absorbed it in a far more real and powerful way than we
could ever imagine.

**What does the suffering of Jesus mean to you? How might
it illuminate your own suffering?**

Verse 19: "All my intimate friends detest me." No passage of
Scripture expresses the loneliness of the sufferer more than this,
verses 13-19. Loneliness is a terrible thing, and has driven many
a person mad! We see it in the life of Jesus as he made his way
to the Cross (Mark 10:32-34), in Gethsemane (Luke 22:39-46),
and in the desolate cry from the Cross, "My God, my God, why
have you forsaken me?" (Matt. 27:45). The New Testament sees
loneliness as being part of the way of the disciple of Jesus (Luke
14:25-27).

**Have you experienced loneliness and rejection in your
own life? Have you experienced either of these as a
consequence of your Christian walk? How do you handle
it? Have you ever tried relating it to the Cross of Christ?
Paul incorporated it into his full understanding of the
Christian way, and of Christian service (Col. 1:24). How
would you understand his words?**

An extended note on verse 25

"There is one God and one mediator between God and men, the man Christ Jesus, who gave himself as a ransom for all men" (I Tim. 2:5-6).

"I know that my Redeemer lives." This magnificent statement of faith provides both a problem and a blessing for the Christian reader. In the first place, as indicated above, within the context of Job's concerns 'Vindicator' is probably a better way of understanding it here. Job wanted someone to defend his cause at the bar of divine justice, and his bold statement of faith is that only God himself can do that. Yet we are so accustomed to using it in a distinctly Christian way that we are likely to confuse application with original meaning. The only coherent way, in terms of the book as a whole, is to understand Job's desire as being for a mediator who will vindicate his cause.

Yet at the same time the word he uses is of wider-ranging significance. The Hebrew noun *go'el* means basically a near relative, and is sometimes translated that way, e.g. in I Kings 16:11, or even "close relative" (Lev. 21:2), or "kinsman-redeemer" (seven times in Ruth 3 and 4). Here is the daring faith of Job, that he even stakes a claim to expect God to act as his near relative who is morally bound to come to his defence!

Now, this same word is also used in contexts where someone is deprived of the normal provisions of life and is reduced to poverty and misery. Thus the Lord is described as Israel's redeemer in the Exodus story, since he brought them out of the misery of slavery. A graphic example of this is found in Proverbs 23:10-11, where the reader is exhorted, "Do not...encroach on the fields of the fatherless, for their *Defender* (Heb. *go'el*) is strong; he will take up their case against you." It is in such a line of understanding of the term that we may place both Job's use of it, and the Christian application of Job's use.

There is always something profoundly new in the Christian focus. Job's use is intensely personal, relating to his own particular need, and perhaps to those who suffer physically, financially and emotionally, as he did. The Christian use is perfectly legitimate in applying it to the whole of humanity. We all stand impoverished before God, our righteousness as filthy rags (Isa. 64:6), as the later prophets came to understand when confronted with Israel's continual tendency to sin, to evil, to breaking their covenant with the Lord. But Israel is not to be blamed particularly, since she is a mirror of us all. In the wider sense we all have a right to see in the Lord our only hope, our only Redeemer before the divine tribunal, but in our case the plea is not for vindication, but for mercy and forgiveness. We throw ourselves on the clemency of the court.

So Christ becomes our only Mediator with God, just as Job longed for a mediator. If and when we sin, "we have one who speaks to the Father in our defence – Jesus Christ, the Righteous One" (I John 2:1). He is our High-Priest in the heavens, who "is able to save completely those who come to God through him, because he always lives to intercede for them" (Heb. 7:25). He is the "Shepherd and Overseer of our souls" (I Pet. 2:25).

15. We live in an unjust world – Chapters 20–21

At this point the account takes on a major new twist. Job has resolved his own problem for the time being, though he will return to it later. This whole section (chs. 20–27) shows that the argument is breaking down. For eighteen chapters we have eavesdropped on a dialogue of the deaf. Job and his friends are on different wavelengths, with irreconcilable differences. The arguments fizz out, but Job will take a new stand, as he paints his own suffering on a much wider canvas: the plight of mankind living in an unjust world. But first we must hear Zophar's final whimper.

Zophar: The mirth of the wicked is brief! – Chapter 20

Poor Zophar. This man, for whom common-sense was the only
redeeming virtue, simply could not understand Job's profound
searching. Indeed he is perplexed by it all. He confesses himself
troubled and disturbed. Vaguely he feels that there is something
in Job's words which implies a rebuke to himself (vv. 2-3).

So he resorts to his only line of defence, an appeal to the
wisdom which can trace its roots back to earth's earliest
inhabitants, the basic theme of which is: "The mirth of the
wicked is brief, the joy of the godless lasts but a moment" (v.5).
For Zophar this is the law on which the foundations of the earth
are laid. Shake that and we have nothing left. He uses brilliant,
graphic, poetical language to say it. Short, pithy, and fitting
sayings pour from his mouth as he describes the guaranteed
destruction of every evil person. But it is no more than he and
his friends have said all along, and the implication is that Job
himself is in just such a position. The sermon ends with the
pompously dogmatic statement, "Such is the fate God allots
the wicked, the heritage appointed for them by God" (v.29).

We live in a world without rules – Chapter 21

In chapter 19 Job had reached a decisive point in which his
own anguished cries had been quietened. He had found the
Mediator who would defend his cause before God – God
himself. So he now turns from his own dilemma to argue the
problem which has constantly niggled in the back of his mind,
the feeling that he is a cameo of humanity in its suffering. He
will now attack his friends' apparently safest citadel: the
retributive justice of God as an absolute fact. He will argue that
that justice is not at all discernible in the real world.

Listen carefully... – read 21:1-6.

Job now follows the procedure laid down in the book thus far,
where each speaker begins by lampooning the previous
discourses of the "enemy". But this introduction takes a step
forward. Job senses that what he is about to say will leave his

friends punch drunk – or rabid! If what he has said up till now has caused them shock, what follows will strike them dumb (v.5). They have spoken frequently of the 'consolations', which they had been seeking to give him through their counsel. Now he assures them that there is only one 'consolation' he needs, and that is for them to listen to him. He demands of them silence, whilst he now gives his discourse, and after he is through with it, they can say what they like, it will have as much effect as water on a duck's back.

It must be remembered that till now Job had been schooled in the same thought patterns as his friends, with their neat little formulas designed to explain all human experience, and God's doings. His thoughts have even rocked his own boat and left him petrified (v.6), but they must be given the full light of day.

What Job is about to say is so decisive, that by the end of the speech he bluntly pours scorn on all that his friends have said, "So how can you console me with your nonsense? Nothing is left of your answers but falsehood" (v.34). To reduce his friends position to baloney and deception is indeed very strong language, but we must hear him out, remembering that even he himself had been shaken by his own thoughts.

Why do the wicked live on? – read 21:7-16
First, he begins by rubbishing the friends' central argument, which Zophar had sought to clarify in his latest speech: "the mirth of the wicked is brief, the joy of the godless lasts but a moment" (20:5). To the friends this is an unalterable law, by which the universe is governed. It is clearly stated in the speeches of Eliphaz (ch. 15) and Bildad (ch. 18). This unalterable law of divine justice is the central plank of the friends' reasoning.

Job now undermines this argument: "Why do the wicked live on, growing old and increasing in power" (v.7)? Implied in this question is the fact that Job's problem does not lie merely with his friends, but with his God. His complaint is directed against the way God seems to have messed up the rules of the universe. The rigid laws of right and wrong propounded by his friends are not discernible in the real world. It is important to note that Job does not say this triumphantly, as one scoring a point in a debate. Basically he holds the same opinion as his friends, but that is the greater part of his distress. That is the way the world should work, but tragically it does not appear to do so.

To prove his point Job treats us to a vivid picture of the prosperity of evil people. He agrees they deserve punishment, as Eliphaz (15:27-30), Bildad (18:5), and Zophar (20:23,28-29) had all affirmed, but the scandal is that God seems to turn a blind eye to them (v.9). Their lives are marked by prosperity (v.10), by happy families (v.11), by great parties (v.12), and by a peaceful death (v.13). They even laugh at God's supposed intervention (vv.14-15). Any reprimand of their way of life is met with scorn. No threat of divine punishment can dent their arrogance.

How often is the lamp of the wicked snuffed out? – read 21:17-21

Job now picks up Bildad's statement in 18:5, turning it from a statement to a question, which expects the answer: rarely. Reality suggests a very different picture. So far from God's anger pouring disaster upon them, he seems to smile amiably at their activities.

Verse 19 would appear to be a popular saying, that even if the wicked aren't punished here and now, it is their children who will reap the consequences. Zophar had suggested this (20:10). For Job this is a cop out, a scandalous affirmation. It is the evil man himself who ought to be punished, not his children. It is of little consequence to him what happens to his children after his death.

The dilemma at the heart of the universe – read 21:22-26

Job is about to say something which strikes at the heart of the supposed absolute justice of God. Before doing so he apologetically concedes that one should not be rash in judging God's actions, that there may be factors in God's administration

Box 16 – A doubting faith.

Having resolved his personal conflict in chapter 19, Job turns to paint his dilemma on a wider canvas – mankind in general. He insists on facing up to life in the real world. He rubs our religious noses into the harsh realities of man's existence. He reminds us of Lovel's famous words, "Truth forever on the scaffold, wrong forever on the throne."

Job's mind is troubled and agitated. His complexity is not that God rules the world unjustly, but that it does not seem to be run on any principles at all! This is the deeper cause of his agony, his doubt of the moral government of the universe. In effect, whilst not pretending to be superior to God (v.22) he says that this is not the way to run a world!

He now lays his cards on the table and indicts God himself for the apparent injustice rampant in the world. Scandalously, it is now God who is on trial. One can imagine Job's friends shaking their heads in furious anger. Yet we should note that essentially he is working on the same principle of retribution as they do, indeed as the key to understanding the world, but that the apparent breakdown of this system causes him intellectual panic: it cannot be that a just God would allow evil men to flourish!

of justice which we cannot expect to understand (v.22).

Nevertheless, this dilemma, which has clearly plagued his mind, strikes at the heart of the concept of divine justice. Here you see a man, Job says, who is born with a silver spoon in his mouth. He never has any need, is never in any danger. Everything in life goes well for him. In contrast, another is born in poverty, and dies in bitterness, never having enjoyed happiness. It reminds me of a TV documentary in which investigators quizzed a debt-ridden, poverty-stricken Brazilian mother of six: "What was the happiest day of your life?" There was an agonizing pause as she searched her memory, and then she whispered, "Perhaps when I die!" Job would have empathized with her agony, as he ends pathetically with the descriptive statement:, "Side by side they (rich and poor) lie in the dust, and worms cover them both" (v.26).

Climax of a devastating critique – read 21:27-34
Job is conscious, obviously, that his friends are waiting for him to get through, so that they can download contradictory arguments against him. He sees it by the anger in their eyes, by their impatient gestures, They are ready to explode with anger, their minds churning over with examples of bad men duly punished. He anticipates their reasoning (v.28).

He is not going to be impressed. Let them ask the man on the street (v.29), where it is recognised that in the real world the wicked are seldom made to suffer for their sins. Of course, so-called wise men, debating with one another in their heated discussions, will theorise on the justice of God, but out there among the common people there is far more realism. So far from this bad man being punished, they will tell you, he goes from bad to worse, and at the end of his life he goes serenely into death, accompanied by the sympathies and applause of his cronies and toadies. It is only the religious man, living in shameful isolation from the real world, who cannot see what is patently obvious.

With this argument Job feels he has finally dealt the death-blow to all his friends' reasonings (v.34). One cannot but help noticing a certain arrogance here. He has got past the personal struggle by battling through to salvation. In this chapter he has projected the whole question onto a wider canvass, and questions the whole of God's dealing with man. It is undoubtedly this arrogance which God attacks in 38:2. Job himself has anticipated God's reaction in verse 22. Nevertheless, he is quite certain that he has reduced his friends' carefully constructed mental edifice to rubble.

Christian Reflections

Verse 7: "Why do the wicked live on, growing old and increasing in power?" He has resolved his personal dilemma in chapter 19. Now his perplexity shifts away from himself to suffering mankind, and the apparent triumph of evil. The prophets spent most of their time blasting against evil people who held the reigns of power, and used it to exploit the weak and under-privileged (Isa. 3:13-15). By contrast Jesus, the incarnate Son of God, became the prototype of weakness and deprivation. Born and nurtured in the lowliest circumstances, he became the leader of a rabble in the eyes of the civil authorities. Eventually, "he was crucified in weakness" (2 Cor. 13:4), but not before he had proclaimed the final triumph of the weak: "Blessed are the meek, for they shall inherit the earth" (Matt. 5:5).

In the conflict of power and weakness, where do you stand? Where do you want to stand? Where should you stand according to God's word? Read Matthew 11:25-30.

Verses 23 and 25: "One man dies in full vigour...another man dies in bitterness of soul." This is a great moral riddle for Job, and ought to be for us! If God is for right and justice, why does evil so often appear to triumph? It is a problem that lies at the very heart of the last book of the Bible, the final word, the book of Revelation. "I saw under the altar the souls of those who had been slain because of the word of God.... They called out in a loud voice, 'How long, Sovereign Lord, holy and true, until you judge the inhabitants of the earth and avenge our blood?'" (Rev. 6:9-10). They are given no immediate reply, but the book follows this theme through to the eventual destruction of evil and the triumph of the Lord Jesus Christ (chs. 19–22).

Have you been perplexed by the apparent triumph of evil? Do you just shelve the problem, or is there something in your armoury by which you are able to confront it? It must surely be one of Satan's chief tools for destroying confidence in the justice of God!

Verse 27: "I know full well what you are thinking..." Job attacks the stubbornness of his friends, their rigidity, their unwillingness to think again, to reflect on his particular case.

Are stubborn traditionalists evident in your circles, whether Christian or secular? What is the strength, and what the weaknesses of the traditionalist? How far dare we think again, and push the boundaries of our faith? What makes people frightened to think deeply of their faith?

16. Eliphaz swipes out angrily – Chapter 22

Eliphaz opens the third round of speeches. His three discourses can be read over against each other. He had begun by being polite and gentle with Job in chapter 4. In chapter 15 he was a disturbed and frightened man. The basis of his religious faith, his trust in God's perfect retributive justice, had been undermined by Job's insistence on his own innocence. By this third discourse he is livid with anger, for Job has devastated everything he ever believed in.

The chapter divides naturally into three parts: verses 1-3 uses the characteristic opening tactic employed by each of the speakers, trying to debunk what Job has said; verses 4-11 are a vicious attack on Job, accusing him of every imaginable sin; whilst verses 12-30 are yet another pious sermon, explaining to Job how to get out of the pit he has dug for himself.

A restatement of Eliphaz' basic argument – read 22:2-3
He can never get away from his fundamental concern for "righteousness": see his first speech at 4:17; his second speech at 15:14-16. Man born of a woman cannot escape this basic question of his standing before God. Given that every human being is corrupted in some way or other, none of us has a right to stand before our Creator. There is truth in this, but in Eliphaz' mind this means that we should grovel before God. To him the universe swivels on this lone hinge. For Job there are other fundamental questions to seek answers for.

Job – a thoroughly evil man – read 22:4-11

This ungodly pagan has dared to cling to the affirmations of his personal integrity. He must be demolished. Eliphaz argues with cold logic. For him there is now not a shadow of doubt, that Job is altogether evil. He turns in blazing anger on the man who has shaken his world, this uncivilised savage who pits himself against all wisdom and tradition and regards nothing as sacred.

"Is it for your piety that he rebukes you?" (v.4). Of course not, it is for your sin. There is no shadow of a doubt now in Eliphaz' mind that Job is experiencing well-merited punishment from God. He proceeds to treat Job to a catalogue of his sins and vices (vv.6-9).

> distrustfulness of those close to him
> heartless exploitation of those in debt to him
> withholding food and water from the needy
> rejecting widows and orphans who sort his help

We can only say that they are lies, **lies, LIES!** *"Orthodoxy accuses those who sin against it, not only of heresy, but of every other imaginable vice. It is fighting desperately to salvage some part of its treasured ideas"* (Hanson).

Eliphaz had previously admitted that Job was a godly man (4:3,4), which in itself proves how shallow his accusations here are. More than anything he accuses Job of exploiting his position of power in society, for the sake of personal enrichment and glorification. Later, Job rejected all these accusations one by one (31:16-19), which shows they had stung him very deeply, but both God's initial statement of Job as blameless and upright (1:8) and Job's own description of his former life (ch.29) give the lie to these accusations. We will not look at these here since a detailed explanation would divert attention from the main thrust of Job's story.

Yet another pious sermon – read 24:12-30

On the positive side the best that Eliphaz can do is to give Job
yet another pious sermon on the Greatness of God (vv.12-20),
terminating with an exhortation to reconciliation with God
(vv.21-30). In verse 21 the NIV's "Submit to God" is more
literally "Agree with God", but what Eliphaz really means is
"Agree with me"! The verse simply reiterates the basic position
of the wisdom school. Prosperity is the natural outcome of piety,
so repent and all will be well. This assumes that Job was guilty.

We could at this point expound this sermon. It is well crafted,
clearly set out, and cleverly illustrated. It states timeless
principles, true in themselves, but their intentional application
to Job as a bad man is clearly wrong. For this reason it would
be pointless to explain the sermon, for it does nothing to clarify
the problems posed by Job and the book.

Christian Reflections

Verses 21-30: "Submit to God and be at peace with him..." This
is Eliphaz' 'Good News' sermon, and it is very striking. I heard
in my youth a striking gospel sermon on this passage by an
outstanding preacher. Read it carefully and you will see it has
all the ingredients for a good sermon: repentance, truth in the
heart, cleansing of the life, putting God in the centre over against
material possessions, and the promise of rich blessings, answered
prayer, etc. But Job will ignore it completely.
**Do you agree with Job ignoring this 'Good News' sermon?
Why? Why not? Would you use it as such yourself?**

17. The heavens are brass, but I will trust –
Chapter 23

Strangely Job does not reply to Eliphaz. In this his seventh discourse there is not the usual counterattack we have come to expect, rather he gives himself to meditating aloud. Chapters 23 and 24 deal with Job's personal affirmation of confidence on the one side and on the perplexity of God's dealings with man on the other.

First Job returns to his personal distress and complaint (vv. 2-7). Whilst chapter 19 had seen him rise supreme in faith in God as his personal Advocate, the present chapter shows that that did not signify an end to his sufferings. Whilst he had solved his intellectual and spiritual problem, he is still sitting on the dung heap, scratching his sores, hated and despised by his former friends, relatives, etc.

Worst of all, there is still no voice from heaven to answer his cry. He still wishes to plead his case before his judge, but to no avail. The heavens are brass (v.3), yet he is convinced that if he can gain an audience from this God who hides himself, he will gain vindication and win his suit (vv. 5-7). God is fundamentally just and good. Job says in effect, "I cannot understand, but I will trust." Again we note that chapter 19 had proved to be both the depths of his distress and the climax of his trust. Chapter 23 continues the spirit of confidence in the midst of pain. He clings to the essential goodness and justice of God, even when experience would seem to deny it.

We must not lose sight of this desire for justice, for the right to defend his cause before an all-wise Judge. Job wants now to know the charges which God is levelling against him, contrary to the barbed innuendoes of his friends, but the silence of heaven and the absences of God in Job's world, are heart-breaking (vv.8-9).

Verse 10 shows Job grasping after a truth which he hardly seems to comprehend – that suffering is a form of testing, of purifying. The Christian may be tempted to grasp at this as a key to the book, but it is not so. Nowhere else does Job return to or develop this theme. Would that he had! Yet it is one of those occasional nuggets we find in the Old Testament, suggestive, inviting, tantalising, but left in cold storage till the new revelation in Jesus will open to our eyes all the latent possibilities enshrined in the idea.

Job drops the subject. All he can do is affirm his basic innocence (vv.11,12). He is utterly convinced that he has never deviated from the path that the Lord had shown him, that his whole life has been marked by a hunger to know God's word and to consume it as his "daily bread".

The chapter, rooted in Job's personal experience, ends with a dark cloud of pain and perplexity (vv. 13-17). God, who carries through his decrees against his one-time servant, is once again Job's opponent, without a word of explanation. Such a God fills our hero with terror, yet he refuses to silence his voice of complaint (v.17).

Christian Reflections

Verse 3: "If only I knew where to find him..." The silence of the heavens increases Job's agony ten-fold. Consider here the Christian truth of the openness of heaven, of the intercession of Christ on our behalf before the throne of the Father. It is a great consolation and inspiration to the Christian to know that at any time, in any set of circumstances, indeed, even in any sin or weakness, he/she has immediate access to the divine presence. **Look at the following verses, and in each case, on what does the writer ground this openness (I John 2:1-2; Heb. 4:14-16; 7:26-27)? What consolation does this bring to your own spirit? Do we need to "feel" this ongoing work of Jesus as our ambassador in heaven, or is it a faith position, often not dependent on what we "feel"?**

Verse 10: "When he has tested me, I shall come forth as gold."
This, of course, lies at the very heart of the Christian
understanding of suffering (I Pet. 1:7; James 1:3; Heb. 12:4-11),
but for Job it was something unheard of, and he drops the subject
immediately, and never explores it again. Paul says that we
should "rejoice in our sufferings", in the same way we rejoice
in the hope of glory (Rom. 5:2-5). In this he is echoing the words
of Jesus (Matt. 5:11-12). See also Hebrews 12:1-2.

**What does this precious verse mean to you? Do you need
testing? Continue the Hebrews passage down through verses
7-13. What elements of testing and suffering in your life could
be described as divine discipline? What objectives is God
seeking to achieve through them? Do you think you are
learning the lessons?**

18. The earth is full of violence – Chapter 24

Job the outcast proceeds to identify with all the outcasts. He
turns again from his own sufferings to those of mankind in
general. His complaint here is that, contrary to all his friends'
arguments, there seems to be no time when God brings in justice
(v.1). One feels the power of Job's argument. Those who love
God look constantly to see justice happen, but often they feel
defrauded (v.1b). In reality the whole earth is full of injustice
and violence (vv. 2-24).

We are reminded here of the Old Testament prophets, but
Job lacks their fiery anger at those who practice evil, and is
rather concerned with a God who permits them to do it. We
might compare it with the dispassionate attitude of the Proverbs,
where injustice and poverty are evil phenomena to be observed.
Here in Job there is an implied protest against the injustice of
letting such things happen, and it is God who stands accused of
indifference. Whatever we might think of Job's conclusions,
his description of human evil is as relevant today as it was in
his day.

Verses 2-12 describe eloquently a suffering mass of humanity, suffering needlessly caused by human greed, exploitation and injustice. It must be the most powerful statement in ancient literature of the way the powerful exploit the weak in human society, what Burns called, "man's inhumanity to man." It begins with the rather unremarkable statement, "Men move boundary stones." We are inclined to interpret this as the crafty nocturnal moving of a boundary stone a metre or two during the night. But if we see it as the plunder of poor people's land altogether, then the statement serves powerfully as a heading to the rest of the passage. Read it in the light of Micah's angry tirade against the powerful: "They covet fields and seize them, and houses, and take them. They defraud a man of his home, a fellow-man of his inheritance" (2:2).

Their clothing is soon reduced to rags, they are forced to take shelter in caves and rocks, whilst their children are snatched from their breasts to be reduced to slavery in order to pay the most trivial debts. Their only living space is some miserable hovel in the nearby city and the passage concludes with one of the most pathetic pictures in the Bible: "The groans of the dying rise from the city, and the souls of the wounded cry out for help. **But God charges no-one with wrongdoing**." As a final outburst, Job indicts God for his apparent indifference to this appalling scene of human abuse and misery.

In chapter 21 we saw the way in which the wicked prosper materially and socially; here Job's thoughts reach out to those on whose head the wicked have trampled in their greed for wealth and power. People have been expelled from their homes and their fields, their animals have been taken from them, by those who hold power, so that they are reduced to being scavengers on the edges of society. The widows and the orphans, the weakest people in society, are particularly the objects of this abuse, so that once proud landowners were forced to shrink to the level of day labourers, working in the fields and vineyards they once owned.

Probably the meaning is that the poor country people,

Box 17 – There is no justice in the world.
Job's inability to understand God's ways with man grow more intense in this chapter. On the one hand Job has resolved his own deep agony. Now the suffering of mankind in general, the apparent lack of justice in the world God has created, and confronted with which God appears to be indifferent, is driving Job crazy.

This wrestling with doubts about the injustice and evil with which the world abounds is very common in the Old Testament. Habakkuk has been shown the evil with which his nation teems (1:2-4), yet, complains Habakkuk, God himself seems indifferent to it. Jeremiah puts the searing question to God himself: "I would speak with you about your justice: Why does the way of the wicked prosper?" (Jer. 12:1). It could hardly be put more bluntly.

Yet there is a difference between the rest of the Old Testament and Job. The prophets get angry with the perpetrators of the injustice, whilst in contrast Job is angry with a God who permits them to do it. Perhaps better to say that Job is not so much angry as emotionally devastated. If we remember that Job will have held the position of his friends, on the absolute justice of God's ruling of the world, which his own experience has knocked on the head, we feel the pathos of his agonized cry: "But God charges no-one with wrongdoing" (v.12).

deprived of their way of living, driven out by greedy landlords, are forced to live in the city, where they are equally mistreated, and where they end their days in misery.

Verses 13-17: There in the city, evil still stalks the unsuspecting poor, this time in the forms of murder, theft and adultery. Criminals carry out their degenerate work safely, under the shadow of darkness. These, says Job, are the scum of the earth (v.18).

Verses 18-25 cause some difficulties. They seem to clash with
everything that Job has said in the previous two speeches
(chapter 21 and the first part of chapter 24). They seem to agree
with the friends that God in his righteousness punishes evil men.
It does take the argument a step further by saying that he lets
them feel secure for a while (v.23), but assures us that very
soon God catches up on them and destroys their lives.

For this reason some think that from this point confusion
crept in, and a later editor of the book tried to rearrange the
order of things, but got them mixed up. So in that case this
passage could be attributed to one of the friends. However, it
may be possible to attribute the passage to Job. He does not
necessarily say that his friends' position is totally wrong. Indeed,
he starts from the same position as they, his disparity being that
they see it as an inflexible rule, while he claims that it so often
does not work that way. As a general statement much of what
they say may be true. It is when they try to squeeze Job into
their straitjacket that they go astray. Moreover, their generalised
explanation of things does not explain much that happens in
the world, before their very eyes.

Christian Reflections

Verses 1-12: "They thrust the needy from the path and force all
the poor of the land into hiding." This is a grim picture of the
abuse of the poor, who are exploited for the enrichment of the
powerful. This is firmly anchored in every level of the Old
Testament, in the law (Exod. 22:21-27), in the prophets (Mic.
2:1-2; 3:1-3), and in its wisdom (Prov. 13:23). Jesus himself
identified with the poor, not only in the way he was born,
nurtured and lived, but also in his preaching. See especially
Luke 6:20-26.

**What do you think should be the Christian's attitude and
activity today on behalf of the poor? How would you define
poverty? Is there much poverty near you? What do you do
about it?**

This passionate chapter reminds me of a cartoon, in which a
Christian says to another Christian, "Sometimes I want to ask
God why he doesn't do something about the poverty, exploitation
and injustice that we see so much of today." His friend says,
"Well, why don't you?" The reply, "I'm afraid he might ask me
the same question!"

Chapter 24 portrays a devastatingly grim picture of human
suffering. Job would have heartily agreed with the saying of the
18th century thinker, Thomas Hobbes, that human life is
"solitary, poor, nasty, brutish, and short". Pictures of the
common people of past times, painted by great painters like
Bruegel, Teniers, Steen and Hoggarth, give grim pictures of
poverty, and its concomitant vices of bawdiness, drunkenness
and idiocy, seem to bear this out. Yet the New Testament tells
us that Jesus came to bring freedom!
   **Would you agree with Hobbes' statement? What is the
freedom Jesus offers? Does it enter into the natural realm?**

The debate ends in confusion

The last discourses of Bildad and Job (chapters 25–28)
The argument at this point is clearly running out of steam. It
has, in any case, been a dispute of closed minds. No one is
willing to budge an inch. The combatants are clearly exhausted,
and the speeches in deadlock. Bildad's response to Job's latest
speech is the briefest of all, and Zophar, whose turn it should
have been at the end of chapter 26, can't think of anything to
say.

19. Bildad's pathetic response – Chapter 25

Bildad's response is pitiful. He does not answer Job, because
he cannot. He is not on Job's wavelength to be able to respond
to him. Instead Bildad limits himself to two points, both of which
have been adequately made before. The one thing he is sure of

is that he does not like Job's attitude, since it lacks reverence for God and indulges in self-justification, which in Bildad's view is impossible for mortal man.

Verses 2-3: Only God can be seen in all his perfection as the supreme one to whom authority, and correspondingly awe on man's part, belong. Evidently Job has shown a singular lack of awe. Yet God's supremacy, and man's self-humbling before him, had long before been affirmed by Job (9:4).

Verses 4-6: Only God is truly righteous, so that for any man to plead his innocence and righteousness before God is clearly wrong. Eliphaz had made this point in his first speech (4:17), and Job had recognized its basic validity in 9:2. It is made just as clearly in other Scriptures: "Do not bring your servant into judgment, for no one living is righteous before you" (Ps. 143:2); "There is not a righteous man on earth who does what is right and never sins" (Eccl. 7:20).

Box 18 – Collapse of the arguments.

Chapters 25–28 are not easy to fit into the general argument. Bildad begins with the shortest speech of the book, apparently unable to get his wits together (ch 25). The next three chapters all appear to be from Job, yet there are passages (26:5-14; 27:8-23) which sound as though they might have been pronounced by the friends, and which seem to contradict Job's earlier arguments.

Furthermore, chapter 28 sounds like a lull in the whole story, designed to let the reader relax a little before Job presents his final discourse. It is more easily understood as the work of the narrator rather than Job.

Whatever we decide about the voices behind these passages, one thing is certain. The arguments have broken down, this dialogue of the deaf has reached its only possible climax – rampant confusion. This prepares us for the final discourse of Job in chapters 29–31 and for the Lord's speech in chapters 38–41.

However, Bildad misses the point. His conviction is that Job's defence is riddled with contradiction, since in agreeing that God alone is righteous, he should have humbled himself in the dust to confess his own degenerate life. Bildad's final jab in verse 6 displays this. In Bildad's eyes, man, every man, and Job in particular, is a maggot and a worm, and thus not entitled to any kind of self-defence before the Almighty.

It is important to note that in the thinking of the friends, man's false claim to innocence before God is set in the context of the majesty of God, whereas usually in the Bible it is set in the context of man's sin and rebellion, and, therefore, his guilt. This is not the matter at issue in the book of Job. Bildad correctly interprets the mentality of the friends with his reduction of man to a maggot and a worm when measured against the majesty of God, and this should be enough for every man to humiliate himself before his Creator.

20. Job's reply to Bildad – Chapter 26

Superficially it would appear that our author attributes the whole of chapters 26–31 to Job, but statements in 27:1 and 29:1 to the effect that Job resumed his speech suggest that they are distinct phases, perhaps separated in time.

Job's sarcastic comeback to Bildad – read 26:1-4
This is the last of Job's stinging rejections of his friends' counsel, and the most powerfully sarcastic. In his condition on the rubbish heap he is powerless and feeble, both in his own feeling, and in their eyes; but so far from helping him, they have only rubbed salt into his wounds. They have aggravated his condition. Their pretended learning has only shown their bankruptcy of true wisdom. Since they have been unable to offer any help to him, weak and ignorant in their eyes, what then must be the source of their words? Certainly not the divine Spirit (v.4).

In praise of divine power – read 26:5-14

Responding to Bildad's affirmation of divine power (25:2-3), Job demonstrates that his understanding of that theme is quite as profound as that of the friends. He acknowledges that nothing is outside God's sight or control, whether in the depths of the grave, or in the star-studded heavens above. Death and what lies within and beyond it are a ceaseless mystery to man, yet to the eyes of God they are totally transparent, "naked before God". This must have been of great consolation to Job who all along has reflected on the awfulness of death. The wonderful truth he had established at the height of his personal search (19:25), that God his vindicator is there even beyond death, must have caused him immeasurable relief.

The reader may well be puzzled by some expressions in this passage. Who is the Rahab of verse 12, cut to pieces by the Lord, and what is the 'gliding serpent' which he pierces? The answer lies in pagan mythology, where creation happened as a result of a bitter conflict among the gods, in which the triumphant one kills the evil one, splitting her (sorry, yes 'her') in half and using the parts of her body to form the universe. The Old Testament often touches on these myths, but always uses them in poetic language, to vividly illustrate the Lord's power over the whole created order. All 'powers', imaginary or real, are under the sovereign control of the Lord. At best such powers are his playthings, they have no real power.

The chapter ends (v.14) with a remarkable statement about the limitations of our understanding of divine power and wisdom. Though he has sketched God's power Job recognizes that we are strictly limited in our ability to comprehend it. This is clearly intended as a rejection of the friends' pretensions to understand God's ways to perfection. At best we can only understand the faintest whisper of his actions; what then would it be like to hear the thunder roll? Surely intolerable and impossible for man to comprehend.

Christian Reflections

Verses 12-13: "By his wisdom he cut Rahab to pieces...his hand pierced the gliding serpent." Verses 5-14 embrace for the last time in this book Job's pathetic preoccupation with death. He speaks of Sheol and Abaddon (v.6), Rahab and the gliding Serpent. See the notes above on the meaning of these. There is something frighteningly sinister about these forces of death as Job understood them. To the Christian, the New Testament assures such of the ultimate victory over all Satanic forces. Jesus claims victory over all principalities and powers, and tells us to go out and proclaim this to all the nations (Matt. 28:18-20). See Colossians 2:15. Jesus' interpretation of history means that his historic mission was to bind the strong man, a figurative description of all that is evil, and to offer freedom to all (Matt. 12:29).

What does Jesus' Victory mean to you? Specifically, from what has Jesus freed you from? See Heb. 2:14-15; Rom. 6:17-18,22; 8:2,15; Gal. 5:1.

21. Innocence and majesty – Chapter 27

A powerful plea of innocence – read 27:1-6
Verse 1 suggests a break with chapter 26. At this point the order of speakers would have required another speech from Zophar. Since he is clearly dumb, Job resumes his discourse. What Job now says brings into strong contrast his own clear-cut conclusions, in contrast to the breakdown of his friends' arguments.

First, he affirms that God has been the author of his months/ years of anguish, and that there is a fundamental denial of justice in God's actions. Verse 2, "As surely as God lives...", is a solemn oath which Job uses to affirm his innocence before God and man. Here is a striking contrast. While protesting against God's apparent injustice, his turning Job's life from sublime happiness to extreme bitterness, nevertheless Job makes his oath of innocence in God's name, with God as his sponsor. Here indeed is his grave dilemma (his inability to understand God's ways) bonded with rock certainty of the love of God. The same God who has made his life bitter, is the One who has sustained him at every moment.

Secondly, Job will never let go his appeal of innocence. He is utterly determined to pursue it to the end, bitter or sweet though that may be (vv. 4-6). He takes a step forward in his argument, the concluding step. To admit that his friends are right, to search his soul for some hidden sin, to grovel before God, to confess it, would in itself be a lie, a denial of Job's integrity. He will never yield on this point. This anchor of his soul is reaffirmed. From the beginning of the arguments till now he has spoken nothing but the truth in defending his own innocence. To admit that they are right would be a downright lie.

Verse 6: There is no way back. He will NEVER retreat from this affirmation of innocence. His life has been an open book, so that no charge has been brought legitimately against him.

Job's hatred of the wicked – read 27:7-23
This passage has caused much discussion among Bible interpreters. It would fit easily into the mouths of any of Job's friends, but sounds harsh in his own. Yet the narrator includes it as a statement by Job. The basic question is whether these ideas are consistent in Job's mouth? It would seem better to retain them as Job's and ask whether they might after all be reconciled, both with what Job has consistently held and with what his friends have said.

It is important to remember that Job's friends were not entirely wrong. Evidence of this may be found in Psalm 37, which boldly affirms the triumph of the righteous and the disaster looming over the wicked: "A little while, and the wicked will be no more...but the meek will inherit the land and enjoy great peace" (v.10). Let us state clearly that this psalm is God's word to us. Its message is true.

Yet in striking contrast, the psalmist in Psalm 73 is not nearly so confident that evil will be punished: "I envied the arrogant when I saw the prosperity of the wicked...(yet) all day long I have been plagued. I have been punished every morning." Clearly the psalmist was in grave trouble, and life was a terrible burden to him, and to look around and see how wicked people seem to go through life unscathed by misfortune was intolerable.

Now both these psalms are, in Christian thought, inspired by God. In some sense they are both God's word to us. In the same way, both Job and his friends state the truth from the angle in which they speak. It is when they state their slant on the truth as an absolute, that they measure reality from a limited, narrow, shortsighted perspective.

There is another interesting parallel between this passage and Psalm 73. The psalmist there begins with the basic theological affirmation that assuredly, "God is good to Israel, to those who are pure in heart." Yet he immediately confessed that life's hard knocks had undermined his confidence in this simple theological statement. Job does the same. In principle he held to the theology of his friends, in divine retribution on evil, not in judgment beyond the grave, but in the here and now. It is their rigid application of the principle, as though it were the key to all mysteries, which infuriates him.

Verse 11: "I will teach you..." From being constantly instructed by his friends, Job now turns the tables on them. He accepts their basic affirmation of the punishment of the wicked, but asserts by implication that though the truly wicked deserve God's wrath, they are wrong in putting Job into this category. They are in danger of putting themselves in it! Verse 12 accepts that they have some light on the subject, but the way they have used it against him is simply "meaningless talk".

Job, then, in verses 13-23, asserts what is positive in his friends' approach, in words which Zophar (20:29) could hardly have improved upon. Where the friends went wrong was, in the first case, using these statements as though they were universally true. Job has clearly refuted this in chapters 21 and 24. In the second case they went wrong in applying it rigidly to Job himself. Note the various ways in which evil makes its consequences felt in society:

- ♦ Children suffer the consequences of their parents' evil (v.14), compare Exodus 20:5;
- ♦ The widow is glad to see the death of her spouse (v.15);
- ♦ He loses his money and property as a consequence of his way of life (vv.16-19);
- ♦ He is subject to mental torment (v.20);
- ♦ He is eventually destined for terminal destruction (vv.21-23).

Christian Reflections

Verse 6: "My conscience will not reproach me as long as I live." Job's claim to a clean conscience before God is the anchor of his thought. How much more is the Christian called to holiness of thought and act? Jesus said, "Simply let your 'Yes' be 'Yes', and your 'No', 'No'; anything beyond this comes from the evil one" (Matt.5:37). What Jesus means by this is that the Christian's integrity should be so clear and transparent that nobody needs to ask for further guarantees. Paul clearly had Jesus' words in mind when writing to the Corinthian Christians. Paul had planned to visit their church, but due to a poisonous spirit invading that community, he had decided against it, with the consequence that they raised questions about his integrity. He replies, "When I planned this, did I do it lightly? Or do I make my plans in a worldly manner so that in the same breath I say, 'Yes, yes' and 'No, no'?" He goes on to tie his personal integrity to that of the gospel he preaches" (2 Cor. 1:17-22).

Lying is the easiest sin of all! How do you measure up? Note that Paul singles out lying as most characteristic of the old nature (Col. 3:9-10). What can be done about it?

Verse 13: "Here is the fate God allots to the wicked..." Some of the ways in which the Old Testament describes God's response to evil, whether person-al or nation-al, can be worded very strongly, even when set in the most glorious devotional setting,

e.g. Psalm 139:19: "If only you would slay the wicked, O God!...
Do I not hate those who hate you, O Lord..." Yet it must be
remembered that some of the strongest words of condemnation
of evil people are found in the words of Jesus, see Matthew 23.

**Do you think there is ever reason for us to be thoroughly
angry with bad people? Give some explicit examples where
the anger of God against evil has fallen, or where you think
it ought to have fallen, but apparently did not. How do you
reconcile this tension?**

22. The search for true wisdom – chapter 28: A Respite from Debate

Chapter 28 is quite unique in this book. It breaks away from the
argument, to sing a song in praise of Wisdom. The song is
unexpected and unannounced. It is in reality one of the greatest
poems of the Bible. The theme is the search for wisdom.

It strikes one as an interlude by the book's author. The
argument has broken down with frayed tempers. We have been
driven on remorselessly for a very long time, and debate has
collapsed in a chaotic muddle. The interlude seeks to calm
things, to cool the temperature of the story, before entering into
the last phase of Job's quest. We shall hear no more of the friends
until the last chapter. From here Job takes centre stage,
presenting his final defence in three stirring chapters (29–31).
From which point we shall expect God's reply.

Though wisdom is often linked to the practical skills of life,
as in the craftsmen who constructed the tabernacle (Exod. 36:1),
here it is concerned with the meaning of life, and the divine
ordering of the world. God alone, the poem assures us, possesses
the key to a total understanding of the world and the human
condition.

The chapter divides naturally into three parts:
1. A graphic picture of ancient mining (1-11);

Box 19 – An interlude – in praise of wisdom.
This chapter is a song in celebration of wisdom, which at
the same time questions man's ability to achieve wisdom
without divine revelation. The chapter hardly seems to fit
in with the debate, except perhaps to affirm the collapse
of arguments based on human wisdom, and to reaffirm
that God is the source and fountain of all true wisdom.

The narrator seems to be saying that the search for
wisdom, personified in the three friends, and even in Job's
own attempts to understand the world, are destined to end
in chaos, for 'The fear of the Lord – that is wisdom, and
to shun evil is understanding?' (v.28). As such it stands
as an interlude, designed to reduce the tension, to conclude
the arguments, and to prepare the way for Job's final
defense.

---

2. The incomparable value of Wisdom over against all
treasures (12-19);

3. Wisdom is to be found only in and by God (20-28).

Ancient mining portrayed – read 28:1-11
Why the lengthy introduction concerning mining? Probably
because it was the latest technology of the age! It was the pride
of man as the ultimate in human achievement, equivalent in
modern times to the moon landing, or the development of the
Internet. By using this ultimate achievement of mankind, the
author sets it over against the truest possible discovery of
mankind – wisdom. The search for wisdom is like the search
for precious metals – hard work, demanding, exhausting,
dangerous, and perhaps unfruitful, but equally often rewarding.

The description of ancient mining to which the author treats
us is quite unique, the oldest and most graphic source of
knowledge of ancient mining. Mines were worked to obtain
silver, gold, iron and copper. The time of the Israelites' entrance

into Canaan was the beginning of the Iron Age. Early on, the Philistines held the knowledge of its technology and thus had the upper hand in conflicts with Israel's early history.

Verse 3 portrays the miner's lantern (more likely a dangerous oil lamp in those days) penetrating the darkness of the bowels of the earth. "Darkness" here is a translation of a phrase, "the shadow of death", indicating the deadliness of the mining enterprise. The miner digs a shaft down into the depths and "dangles and sways" down the shaft. Ancient mining methods were primitive, using footholds in the sides of the shaft, or being lowered by ropes. It was clearly very dangerous work. Man, says our narrator, in his frantic desire for progress exposes himself to difficult and dangerous conditions.

On the earth's surface, farmer, hawks, falcons and wild beasts move, oblivious of the achievements of man beneath feet or flight. One feels here the sense of awe felt by the author trying to describe this latest act of technological greatness achieved by man. Then again, the miner is "assaulting the flinty rock", digging tunnels, and bringing out the treasure. It is this treasure alone which is the meaning of all this hard, dangerous, thankless work. But if he obtains it he will judge that it was all worthwhile. It is easy to see the parallel which the author feels with man's search for wisdom. If man is so adventurous in the search for earthly treasures, how much more ought he to be in the search for wisdom. This chapter thus represents a vivid picture of the wise man's quest.

The unique value of wisdom over against all human treasure
– read verses 12-19

The search for wisdom, our author goes on to say, is infinitely superior to that of the miner searching for earthly treasure. The theme of the chapter is set out in verses 12 and 20: "Where can wisdom be found?" If man can give such incredible effort to the search for earthly metals, how much more effort ought he to put into the search for wisdom. Yet he is totally baffled in his search for it (v.13). Our author then ransacks the vocabulary of the ancient world, spelling out the treasures – gold, silver, onyx, sapphires (probably lapis lazuli), crystal, jewels, coral, jasper, rubies, topaz – for which man will risk life and limb, dismissing each one as utterly inferior to the rich treasures of wisdom.

Wisdom is to be found only in God – read verses 20-28
Our author returns to the theme of verse 12. Where is wisdom to be found? It is a rhetorical question which expects the answer, "nowhere". Neither man, nor beast, nor bird knows of its whereabouts, only God knows (v.23). Verse 24 indicates that his is a bird's eye view of the whole meaning of life, of understanding, of wisdom. Man, individually or collectively, has only a worm's eye view of reality. Yet man need not despair. God is in full control of the earth and the universe (vv.25ff). Man's inability to understand and govern his environment does not imply that God has let the world get out of control. He is still in command.

The chapter ends with two glorious verses. Verse 27 employs four verbs to graphically picture God working at wisdom like a skilled craftsman. He looks, appraises, confirms and tests it. The work of his wisdom, by which he has created all things, is flawless, so that he is able to declare it "very good", as he had in the creation narrative of Genesis 1. Like a master craftsman he knows it inside out in all its manifold complexity.

In the light of that he addresses himself to man with the supreme offer: "The fear of the Lord that is wisdom, and to shun evil is understanding."

The chapter concludes that, though hidden from man's finite mind, wisdom is offered to him if he will submit in humility before his Creator. Parallel to this humility and awe before God is the necessity for hating evil and avoiding it at all cost. In the Old Testament, at every level, these two realities go hand-in-hand – humility before God, and hating evil. They are the essence of the good life, the truly wise life. Conversely, where the fear of God is lacking, evil runs riot. Compare Proverbs 3:7: "Fear the LORD and shun evil," and 8:13: "To fear the LORD is to hate evil."

At this point we have reached one of the great highs of the book of Job. He himself had been just such a man, as the Lord pointed out to the Satan in 1:1, 8: "a man who fears God and shuns evil". But if this looks back to the early chapters, it also anticipates the Lord's reply to Job in chapters 38–41, for it drives home to Job that his search for understanding is ultimately futile, since wisdom "is hidden from the eyes of every living thing... God...alone knows where it dwells" (vv. 21, 23). Part of the objective in the latter chapters is to drive this reality home to Job. He has spent a lot of time criticising the way God runs the universe; now Job must become profoundly conscious of his own limitations in understanding.

Christian Perspectives

Verses 1-11: "There is a mine for silver..." This is an impressive description of the very earliest mining techniques, and it is played out in detail. The objective of such a detailed explanation is found in the comparison it makes with the search for wisdom (v.12): "But where can wisdom be found?" This is an excellent example of the use of imagery to teach truth, which is so characteristic of the Bible. It says – the miner gives his all at great personal cost and danger in his search for silver and gold, how much more self-denying ought to be our search for wisdom?

Since the Bible is so full of imagery, it raises the question of how far such language is relevant to us today. Can we reinterpret it? More: how far are we conscious that the language we are reading is poetic and imaginative, rather than slavishly literal? What does this teach us about the way we handle the Bible?

Verse 28: "The fear of the Lord – that is wisdom, and to shun evil is understanding." These words are a resumé of the basic teaching of the Wisdom schools in ancient Israel. They supply the basic framework of the book of Proverbs, *magnum opus* of the Wisdom movement: "The fear of the LORD is the beginning of knowledge...fear the LORD and shun evil" (Prov. 1:7; 3:7). For the Christian, Jesus himself is the key of access to wisdom:

"in whom (Jesus Christ) are hidden all the treasures of wisdom and knowledge" (Col. 2:3).

In what way is Jesus the source of wisdom for us? What does the word "hidden" mean in this context? How can we "discover" this hidden treasure? In what way does the extensive teaching of Jesus, contained in four Gospels, contain the wisdom we need for daily living?

23. Job presents his concluding defence –
Chapters 29–31

This three-chapter speech is Job's final defence. It divides easily into three parts,

Chapter 29: Job sketches the happiness and glory of his past life;

Chapter 30: Job vividly describes the misery of the present;

Chapter 31: Job exonerates himself of all guilt, which might make him worthy of such suffering.

The reader of the book could well begin with chapters 29 and 30. They are marked by the "language of deep pathos". Job's longest speech sounds to us very much like the counsel for the defence making his last plea to the jury. There will have been no jury in his day, so he argues his own case before God his judge. Job is about to dispute his long-pending lawsuit in eloquent language. This was what his friends had always feared, and must have made them very angry.

The intimate friendship of God – read 29:2-6.
This is a lovely picture of his early life. He can testify that till struck down with this disaster, he had enjoyed the unabated companionship of God. It is important to note here that he recognizes that it is 'the Almighty' (see Box 6) who had blessed his early life, thus establishing the unity of the two faces in which he has seen God. The God who had blessed and enriched his life over so many decades is the same who more recently has smashed him to pulp. Throughout his years he has known

---

Box 20 – Job makes his final defence.

Now that the debate has dwindled and collapsed, Job makes his final defence. First, he spells out the life he enjoyed before this disaster struck him (chapter 29). This is a superb picture of a thoroughly good man. Perhaps, apart from the Gospels' portrayal of Jesus, it could be said that this is the finest picture of what God is looking for in the life of a good man.

Secondly, in chapter 30, Job pictures his present state, after months of sheer agony and torment. He sits miserably on the rubbish heap, his skin blistered and cracked by the sun, a broken man, in whose face people spit, and of whose plight the drunkards sing to hoots of laughter.

Finally, Job approaches his judge spelling out in detail all the possible offences he could be accused of, clearing himself of them, and demanding from God the spelling out of the charges against him. Failing this, Job should be declared innocent (chapter 31).

---

the presence of the Lord as his lamp and light in the midst of the dark passages of life.

He passionately longs for those days to return. The nostalgic touch includes the time when his children were around him. But tragically they were killed at the beginning of his disasters.

Verse 6 uses highly poetic language to describe the supreme good, the beautiful life, the superbly happy years which Job had enjoyed, prior to his disasters. Rivers of oil from the rock, a strange figure to us, yet so common in ancient life. Olive oil was basic to everyday life, and presses were cut as cavities in rock in order to hold it.

The profound respect of his townsfolk – read 29:7-10 with 21-25

If on the one side, Job could look back to that supremely happy life of God's blessing on himself and his family, on the other he could speak of his position in the town community in which he lived, and, let it be said, which had now rejected him. The gate of the city was the hub of social life, a kind of mixture of market place, recreation centre, and town hall. The life of the city revolved around it. Whenever Job appeared there a hush fell over the crowd. People stepped back to let him pass to his honoured seat, whilst the elders of the city rose in respect of his person.

Look now at verses 21-25 which revert back to this theme. Whatever the problem of the town, collective or individual, everyone waited to hear Job's advice, which was so packed with truth, virtue and goodness that there seemed nothing more to be said. As he left, his smile would fall on ordinary people, who would be thrilled to think that he had recognized them. The passage then closes with Job pictured as living supreme among his fellows, "as their chief...as a king...". His position does not seem to have been an official one, an office by appointment, but as one he had gained by the value of a highly respected life.

How to gain respect and admiration – read verses 11-17

The way in which Job had gained this profound admiration and respect is set out in these verses. It gives us what is probably the best biblical sketch of the life of a thoroughly good man, apart of course from that of Jesus in the Gospels. If Job enjoyed respect from his contemporaries it was a respect won by the quality of his life. Commentary ran the rounds in his town, and in neighbouring towns, that spoke of the excellence of that life (v.11). Note the 'because...' in verse 12.

What we have then is a description of what that quality of life consisted in. It was a life dedicated to doing good to everyone, especially the weak: the poor, the orphans, the dying man, the widow, the blind, the lame, the needy, and even those who were strangers to his town. The man who was dying blessed Job (v. 13), because it would seem Job assured him that his widow and children would be cared for, a promise which in turn "made the widow's heart sing" for joy.

These weak people were subject to predators, as Job himself had spelt out in 24:2-12, who ruthlessly sought to bleed them of what little possessions and wealth were theirs. He pictures these grasping people as wild, fierce animals. When he held the reins of power in his community, Job broke their jaws and forced them to release their prey. Too often the poor were exploited by those who held power, for their own enrichment and material comfort. Not so by Job.

In fact, Job tells us that his actions were motivated by 'righteousness' and 'justice' (v.14). These two words are used more than 1,000 times in the Old Testament, very often together. They have been called inseparable twins. Basically they mean that the law was to be performed by thoroughgoing goodness, and that goodness was to be determined by the biting edge of law. That is why the Old Testament insists so much on these qualities. Job had determined to direct his life, not by personal enrichment and personal fulfilment, but by serving the weak among his people. It was this that caused such a deep impression on his fellow citizens.

In this Job follows closely in the footsteps of Moses and of the prophets, who continually stressed the need for those in power to stand by the side of the weak and poor. Too often, those in power abused their strength to exploit the weak, so as to further their own material interests.

Visions of a happy retirement – read verses 18-20.
Having lived such a supremely happy and good life, Job expected that the latter years of life would be rewarding to him in his old age. That dream had been shattered by the experiences spelled out in chapters 1 and 2. Dying "in my own house" means surrounded by his wife and children, and grandchildren. But now his children are dead, his wife has rejected his company, and he has been expelled from the town by those very people among whom he had lived as "king".

Did ever a man have such a right to be miserable? Job

expected his life in old-age to be like a fruit-bearing tree, green, fertile, yielding sweet fruit to those around him. He had thought that the popularity and respect which were his in life would be his right through to death. Now he sits on the rubbish heap, surrounded by rats and vermin, hated by his former friends, despised by old enemies, a rejected old man.

Christian Reflections

Verse 21: "Men listened to me expectantly, waiting in silence for my counsel." Here we have a double challenge. The picture of a thoroughly good man and of true leadership in a community. Goodness and leadership do not easily blend, for the leader is often too preoccupied with himself, and in taking personal advantage of his position. There are many statements about quality of life in leadership in the New Testament, which are contrary to the pattern of this world, but perhaps the most important is that expounded by Jesus: "You know that the rulers of the Gentiles lord it over them, and their high officials exercise authority over them. Not so with you. Instead, whoever wants to become great among you must be your servant, and whoever wants to be first must be your slave" (Matt. 20:25-27).

How does this picture measure up to your idea of piety and goodness? Does it say anything about going to church, reading your Bible, prayer? What does this say to you about your personal piety? It is of interest to note what the psalmist reminds the king of his day of the true values to be displayed in leadership (Ps. 72:12).

Verses 18-20: "I thought, 'I shall die in my own house...'" Here is Job's picture of a comfortable and enjoyable old age. As I write this I am three weeks into retirement. I am in a comfortable home, which is mine. I have a loving, caring wife, four super grown-up children, and am typing this on a computer in a very spacious study. Really, I've never had it so good! Such a retirement was what Job was longing for, but now we encounter him sitting on the garbage heap, seeing this as his last "home" before death, rejected by the very community which ought to

have ministered to his every need in gratitude for all he had
done in their midst. Jesus was concerned for his widowed mother
even as he hung on the Cross and commended her to the care of
his beloved disciple John (John 19:25-27). Paul gave instructions
for the care of widows who were financially deprived in their
old age (I Tim. 5:3-10).

**What are your visions of retirement, assuming you are
near enough to think about that? What do you think should
be the Christian's care for the aged? What of those of your
own family? of your church? of your neighbourhood
community?**

24. Now they mock me! – Chapter 30

The past, lived within an adoring community, was glorious,
but Job now spells out the misery of the present. This must
surely be the most pathetic chapter of the book. The people
who reject him are the very ones who honoured and respected
him in chapter 29. He is the object of their contempt and ridicule.
We must remember that he must have presented a hideous
appearance, riddled with sores and scabs, over his face as much
as anywhere else, his skin blistered and blackened, sitting
day-after-day on the dung heap outside the city.

"A base and nameless brood" – read 30:1-8,
These have made Job the special object of their scorn. These
are clearly the riffraff, the dregs of society, perhaps even people
living outside the law. Were they the same people for whom
Job wept in chapter 24, who had been initially driven out of
society by cruel and heartless exploitation? These are probably
the second generation. As their condition degenerates through
the ravages of poverty, they become reduced to a group
depending on evil means to scrape an existence on the dung
heap of life. Finding Job in a similar condition, but who has

formerly been one of the ruling class, they turn their venom on him.

They have so made Job the object of their hatred, that in their drunken pub crawls they invent songs about him, stinging mockery. He becomes for them an object of general scorn. When needing to go by him, they take the opportunity to spit in his face. On the other hand, the town leaders make no attempt to rescue him from them, and meet his appeals to them with lofty silence (v. 28).

But behind the rabble Job sees the hand of God. They are another weapon forged by his hand to humiliate Job and increase his misery (v.11). So he continues to see that face of God which speaks of enmity, in spite of the greater vision of God as his friend and saviour in chapter 19. We sense the feeling of total despondency returning to torment his mind (vv.16-23). He is tormented both physically and mentally. It is so easy in the thrust of the debate during the previous long discourses, to forget that filthy heap of human waste on which it is carried out, to forget that not for one moment does Job's distress decrease. Indeed it increases.

Notice the reference to the night pains (v.17). In the night we expect relief from pain, and modern medicines offer us considerable hope in this respect, but for Job it was the onslaught of increased pain and misery, physical and emotional. Again he sees this as the hand of God, showing no mercy, thrusting his face further into the mud (v.19).

Job's only response is to turn to God in prayer, crying out for relief from his misery (v.20). Instead God "turns on me ruthlessly". He drives Job with fury, like the wind whipping up nature's debris. God has removed all restraint, and the only possibility for Job is, once again, to stare into the jaws of death, which is waiting to consume him (v.23). He reaches this point in nearly all his discourses. Death is the only option. It never occurs to him to think of the possibility of restoration to his former state.

A miserable old man – read 30:24-31.

The picture of Job's present condition concludes with a final sight of the pathetic old man collapsing in exhaustion, pain and misery on the refuse heap. He is, in his own words, a broken man (v.24), where the phrase is more literally 'a ruinous heap', perhaps seeing in the stinking dung heap on which he lives a picture of his own life and destiny. He cries for help, expecting at least crumbs of comfort, but he is refused by wife, friends, townsfolk, and God. This seems to Job poor return for the very noble life of helping those in distress which he had practised (vv.25-26).

"I go about blackened" pictures the drab, squalid clothes of mourning, which the bereaved were expected to wear. Verses 29–31 ends with a sad, pathetic picture. Job has become a brother of jackals, whose howl in the night sounds like a cry of desolation. Compare Micah 1:8: "I will weep and wail; I will go about barefoot and naked. I will howl like a jackal, and moan like an owl." Job's skin has turned black, due to his festering sores, his feverish heat, and the merciless burning of the desert sun. Here there is no sheltering hospital bed, only the stench of refuse.

Job ends the chapter with a beautifully poetic, yet pathetically devastating, picture, his harp tuned only to mourning, his flute to the sound of wailing in death, which is all he can hope for. We are tempted to weep with this outcast. Perhaps he represents all those who suffer for no known reason.

Christian Reflections

Verse 10: "They detest me...they do not hesitate to spit in my face..." Is Job a picture of Jesus? The picture of his suffering sounds very similar to those of our Lord. Compare Psalm 69:7,12, a psalm quoted extensively in the Gospels in relation to Jesus' sufferings: "I endure scorn for your sake, and shame covers my face. I am a stranger to my brothers.... Those who sit at the gate mock me, and I am the song of the drunkards." In a sense all biblical heroes offer us a shadow of Jesus; imperfect, blotched and defaced, but bearing some semblance to him. We may feel that Job's complaint in the midst of suffering are unworthy to compare with the embracing of the divine will on the part of Jesus. Yet even Jesus prayed in the last night of his life, that were it possible the cup of suffering might be taken from him.

Meditate on the physical sufferings of Jesus, and also on his mental pain. What do these say to you about the heart of God? How do they illuminate your own suffering?

Verse 20: "I cry out to you, O God, but you do not answer." Again we return to the silence of God, which is a critical part of Job's deep agony. Why doesn't God respond? Again we note the similarity with Jesus, as he cried from the cross, "My God, my God, why have you forsaken me?" Why the silence of God? Surely because there is no cheap answer to our agony. God does not spring to our aid the moment we cry out, for he has deeper purposes to achieve in the midst of our distress.

The apostle Paul expounds one of the greatest functions of suffering – to transform us into missionaries of human empathy! He had recently passed through a traumatic experience: "We were under great pressure, far beyond our ability to endure, so that we despaired even of life. Indeed, in our hearts we felt the sentence of death" (2 Cor. 1:8,9). From this he learned valuable lessons. First, that "this happened that we might not rely on ourselves, but on God"; secondly, that their deliverance was a guarantee of future protection. But thirdly, and most importantly, in the midst of distress he had found divine comfort, from "the Father of compassion and the God of all comfort who comforts us in all our troubles, *so that* we can comfort those in any trouble with the comfort we ourselves have received from God" (read 2 Cor. 1:3-10). Having experienced the divine comfort, we are liberated from our selfishness, our self-sympathy, to enable us to empathise with those who suffer.

Have you experienced God's comfort in some distressing situation? Did you think that God was allowing you to pass through it in order to train you up as a comforter of others? What would this mean to you today?

25. Job's final defence in court – Chapter 31

Job's head is battered, but unbowed. Scourged and bruised he may be in chapter 30, but he stands with head erect to be counted at the coming tribunal.

We have seen how Job began his final defence in chapter 29, describing vividly his former comfortable life, his place in society, his high standing, his personal integrity, his concern for the weak and the poor of the town. He then went on to describe the condition of misery to which he had been reduced, and for which there could be no justification.

Now, in chapter 31 he concludes his plea. The essence of this chapter is expressed in the words: *"I sign now my defence"* (v.35). This is the climax, an effort to reassert the integrity he has appealed to throughout the argument. His manner of doing this is intriguing.

He calls down upon his own head solemn curses. He is a broken man, an outcast, deserted by God and loathed by men, but he intends to vindicate himself, and he does so vigorously. He has pled for an audience with God, has begged God to spell out the sins which merited this suffering. But the heavens are brass. So in the non-appearance of his Accuser, Job clears himself with solemn oaths, listing all conceivable crimes and calling for dreadful penalties. This was current courtroom procedure.

Were Job to receive the accusations in writing, it would resolve his problem. He would be able to bear a just accusation, in fact he would wear it boldly, proclaiming it to all (v.36). It is his present suffering which has no basis in justice, of which his Creator is the author, which is intolerable to Job.

The chapter begins by stating that at some stage Job had "made a covenant with my eyes not to look lustfully at a girl" (v.1). That he should begin his list of sins meriting divine judgment with this, suggests that it had been a real battle for him at a decisive point in his experience, perhaps in his youth. That he had made a covenant about it means that he had entered into a solemn promise before God to maintain sexual purity in thought as well as action. What a lesson this is for the modern age. Job's energies became devoted to serving his fellow men rather than indulging his own lusts. Would that our modern leaders were more concerned for the former than the latter!

This covenant is undergirded by a most important reasoning (vv. 2-4). Job knows that he is a man accountable to God, that God observes a man's every step, and that there is a punishment, 'ruin' and 'disaster', for those whose mode of life displeases God. Thus what undergirds all the moral standards set out in this chapter – and the chapter is almost a summary of the Bible's values – is the thought of one's responsibility to God and his power to punish the sinner, which serves as a constant deterrent in Job's life. Without such a set of beliefs there cannot be a deterrent to evil.

Job now sets out a number of curses, which he calls down upon himself if he has transgressed the moral laws. There are six curses, which Job evokes on his own head with the "If...then" formula. This happens in each of the six curses and was normal legal procedure.

Deceit (vv.5-8). Notice that the "If..." of verse 5 is matched by the "then..." of verse 8. But note that there may be a number of "if"s, but normally only one "then". Even this may be at times understood rather than stated, e.g. verses 13-15. Here in verses 5-8 the appeal is to total integrity of heart and action. There has been nothing hidden to the eyes of others in Job's lifestyle. This being the first of the curses may be said to undergird all the rest. It is not merely for overt actions that Job claims innocence, but also to inward disposition, the thought life. His was an inward integrity, essential to his belief that under divine scrutiny he would be found not guilty (v.6). Again it is important to notice that in this chapter the crimes spelt out are not those of criminal activity, but of a going astray from the positive elements of goodness.

Immorality (vv. 9-12). Job here affirms and defends his high estimation of the marriage relationship. This is the logical

Box 21 – Job throws down the gauntlet.

Chapter 31 is the climax of Job's defence. God's dealings with Job, set out in chapter 30, imply that he has already been judged and condemned out of court. But in his mind this is a gross injustice. So here he sets out his appeal, based on a ancient custom of civil courts, where the wronged person requests a hearing with written evidence.

As his defence at law he spells out all the possible crimes of which he might be accused, and solemnly calls down curses on his own head if any such can be proved. Each one carries an "If.... then" formula. In spelling them out Job's desire is: "Let God weigh me in honest scales and he will know that I am blameless" (v.6).

In verse 35, he concludes, "I sign now my defence." Now it is the obligation of his accuser, the silent God, to "put his indictment in writing". Job has done all in his power to clear his name, to plead with God for a clarification of the issue. The silence of the heavens aggravates Job's agony. Now he is prepared, were he to be successfully accused, to "wear it [the indictment] on my shoulder, I would put it on like a crown." We wait with baited breath for God's reply.

extension of the sexual 'covenant' of verse 1, probably a pre-marriage promise, which he had then carried into his married life. For Job there was only one woman to whom he could give his undivided affection, the wife of his youth. To do anything else would have been 'shameful', meriting the fire of hell. The Bible does not trivialise immorality. It is a deadly sin meriting divine judgment of the worst kind! It is in fact 'shameful', i.e. meriting condemnation in the eyes of the world. Tragically we have to confess that in our modern society evils like these are paraded by many as though they were virtues.

In fact, Job spells out the kind of judgment it deserves (v.10). The adulterer's wife, probably reduced to poverty by the lustful husband's immorality, is forced into providing for her own children by doing the most menial tasks for another man, grinding his corn. For Job, seeing his wife reduced to such a condition would have been the ultimate disgrace of his own life.

Injustice (vv.13-15). Job defends the right of his slave to an appeal against his master in a court of law. This is quite remarkable. It is the first case in ancient history where a master defended the right of his slaves to an equal hearing before law, the right to complain against his master. It also shows that Job's religious faith in a divine Creator who had made them both, master and servant, asserted their equality in his way of thinking. Justice is one of the great themes of the Old Testament. An authority on ancient slavery states: "The first person in the ancient Near East who raised his voice to condemn slavery as a cruel and inhuman institution was Job. His was a condemnation based on the moral concept of the inherent brotherhood of man" (G.E.Mendenhall).

Exploitation of the weak (vv.16-23). In his last speech, Eliphaz had accused Job of exploiting the poor by abusing his power (22:5-9). This had clearly stung Job, so he now proceeds to call down curses on his own head if there is any truth in Eliphaz' accusations. Job singles out the widow, the orphan, the poor and the unemployed as the special objects of his concern and care. If he has neglected these needy people, then it would be perfectly just for his arm to be broken off. He later intertwines concern for the poor with other curses, specifying the hungry who ate at his table, and the stranger to whom he gave lodging (vv. 31-32). Again we see that biblical tendency to place its heroes on the side of the poor and rejected of this world. Verse 23 shows again that accountability before God was the motivating spring of all Job's social and moral attitudes and actions.

Covetousness (vv. 24-28). Eliphaz in his last speech had implied that Job's heart had been turned from God by his devotion to his wealth (22:24-25). The love of money had broken his fellowship with God. Job vigorously rejects that insult. Desire for material gain was never among his motives, though he had very much opportunity for it. Chapter 1 had painted Job as an exceedingly rich man, but he had never let this become the centre of his happiness. Wealth brings comfort, prestige before men, and power to achieve whatever one wants. Job had seen his material wealth as a means of serving God.

Idolatry (v.26f.) is singled out and firmly rejected as unfaithfulness to God.

A series of evils (vv. 29–34 and 38-40). In conclusion Job strings together a number of possible evils he might be accused of and calls heaven to account for his integrity: gloating over the downfall of his enemies, seeing it as the result of his own curse (vv.29-30); refusing hospitality to strangers (vv.31-32); the concealing of secret sins (vv.33-34); mistreatment of his tenant farmers (vv. 38-40).

Job interrupts these curses with an agonised plea for the charges against him to be specified (vv.35-37, see Box 21). He has signed his defence, and now calls on his accuser – God – to put his indictment in writing. If only Job knew what the charges were, he would wear the accusation in public for all the world to see. This is part of his great agony – the silence of God, his accuser.

An extended note on 31:35-37

This is an enormously important "parenthesis". It is unfortunate that it should be included in brackets, for this is Job's final thrust, and explains what he is doing, and what he is seeking to achieve, in the whole of chapters 29–31.

It is cast in the language of the law courts. This discourse constitutes his "defence" before God. Actually the word "defence" is not there in the Hebrew. The statement depends on the word "sign", and the "signature" must not be understood in the modern sense. It was most probably a seal. The only other certain use of the word appears in Ezekiel 9:4,6, where the angel is told to "put a *mark* on the forehead" of the mourners.

Job feels he has made a thoroughly adequate self-defence, and puts his seal to it.

Very much earlier in the debate Job had declared his intention to present a defence. As early as 13:3 he had declared: "I desire to speak to the Almighty and to argue my case with God." And a few verses later he affirms, "I will surely defend my ways to his face," and again, "Now I have prepared my case, I know I will be vindicated." Clearly Job had, at a very early stage, thought through carefully the elements he would include in his defence.

God, especially Shaddai (see Box 6), is Job's Accuser. There is a certain conflict here in Job's mind. Early on he had toyed with the idea of bringing his own lawsuit against God (9:3, 14), but quickly dismissed this: "if it is a matter of justice, who will summon him?" (v.19). So the best Job can do is to prepare his defence for presentation at his coming trial. Yet here also is his grave problem, since God issues no summons to him. The heavens are shut tight, and in the whole debate God's voice is not heard.

Now Job throws down the gauntlet to God. Job has done his utmost. He has put his defence in writing and authenticated it with his seal. Now, "Let Shaddai answer me; let my accuser put his indictment in writing." If God were to do this, if he would elaborate the "charges", Job would sense an immense relief. It is the silence of the heavens which deepens his distress. Again this was part of his agony from the beginning, "I will say to God: Do not condemn me, but tell me what charges you have against me" (10:2). Now he positively demands, in a lawsuit setting, that God specifiy the charges.

This is in many ways the resumé of Job's pleas throughout the book, and with this Job concludes his defence.

Christian Reflections

Verses 2-4: "What is man's lot from God...? Is it not ruin for the wicked, disaster for those who do wrong?" The exceptionally

good life which Job had set out for us in chapter 29 was
undergirded by a belief in God's displeasure with evil. In verses
13-15 Job even makes it the basis of his relationships with his
servants, "If I have denied justice to my servants...what will I
answer when called to account?" Accountability before God
was the ground of Job's every action. This was not a threat
hanging over him, as some have portrayed it, but a healthy sense
of personal responsibility toward all with whom he had dealings.

The New Testament affirms that "Man is destined to die
once, and after that to face judgment" (Heb. 9:27), and "we
must all appear before the judgment seat of Christ, that each
one may receive what is due to him for the things done while in
the body, whether good or bad" (2 Cor. 5:10). In the latter case
Paul uses this to explain the motivation of his whole life and
ministry: "We make it our goal to please him (God)...for we
must all appear..."

**Is it of any concern to you that you will one day render
account of your life to God, to Christ? Can you think of any
attitude taken, decision made, etc., which has been influenced
by this consideration? How ought it to influence us?**

Verse 9: "If my heart has been enticed by a woman..." From
verse 1 we learn that this had been a problem for Job, and he
had had to put a strict rein on his carnal desires! It is impressive
that Job should single this out as the first on his list of possible
evils to be condemned! One can only admire his frankness,
though also his moral integrity. Christians are even more
emphatic in their condemnation of immorality and adultery.
Thus Paul exhorts us "that each of you should learn to control
his own body in a way that is holy and honourable, not in
passionate lust like the heathen, who do not know God" (1 Thess.
4:4-5).

**In striking contrast, many of our political leaders, our
sports heroes, our artists, our pop entertainers, withdraw
all restraints and indulge in every kind of fornication and
adultery which attracts them, and this is vividly portrayed
for us on our TV and internet screens. How does this glut of
sex affect you? What do you/will you do to counteract its
influence?**

*The suspense at this point is terrific. God can scarcely ignore
this summons to present his evidence in writing. We stand on
tiptoe to hear God's immediate response.*

Box 22 – What shall we make of Elihu?

We are brought to the point in chapter 31 where we expect
that now most certainly the Lord will answer Job, who
has thrown down the gauntlet to him, so that it is
impossible for God to remain silent. Incredibly this does
not happen; instead Elihu, a young aristocrat who has been
listening in on the debate, intervenes without introduction
and without being invited.

His speech is long-winded – he uses twice the space
of any other speaker, including God. There seems to be
evidence that the others tried to interrupt his flow of words,
but he would not cede space for one moment. At the end
of his speech he got so wound up that he waffles on about
the weather! When he is finished everybody ignores him.

Elihu's defenders insist that he adds something new
to the debate, but I can see little that is new. While he
claims he will not use the friends' arguments, that is
precisely what he does, affirming that Job is being
punished for an evil life. He is even more scandalised
than the friends for the way in which Job has defended
himself and declared God's justice void.

Why Elihu, then? He is the narrator's device, designed
to build up the suspense before the supreme moment of
the story. We were on the edge of our seat, convinced
that after Job's throwing down the gauntlet in chapter 31,
God would have to speak. But the writer introduces the
long speech of Elihu, making us wait impatiently for the
climax of the story.

26. The Speech of Elihu – Chapters 32–37
Wise man or fool?

Elihu is a young aristocrat (only he is given a pedigree) who
has been listening to much of the debate and, the arguments
having fizzled out, now intervenes, uninvited, to give four
successive speeches, to none of which does Job, or anyone else,
respond, probably because Elihu had no intention of permitting
them..

The narrator explains (32:1-5), and Elihu himself expounds,
the reasons for his intervention. As he has listened to the debate
he has been infuriated by two things. First, the plea of innocence
on the lips of Job. In this Elihu stands squarely on the side of
the friends. But on the other hand he is furious with the three
friends for their inability to convince Job of his guilt. Elihu is
superbly confident of his own ability to do that, so that his one
supreme objective is to convince Job of his damnable error.

In respect of Job, Elihu makes five accusations, which show
that he has been in early on the debate, and that he has clearly
understood the drift of the argument.

♦ Job's false claim of innocence (32:2; 33:9; 34:5)

♦ His charge, implicit and explicit, that God has become
his enemy, and has wronged him (33:10-11)

♦ His claims that the heavens are closed to him, that God is
deaf to his cries (33:13)

♦ His questioning of the whole nature of God's justice in
the world in general (34:10-12)

♦ That Job's attacks on God's justice show that Job has
abandoned true religion and has become a companion of
the scum of the earth (34:36-37).

In 35:14-15 Elihu shows singular clarity of thought in summing up Job's two main protests about God: first, that he has presented his personal case before God, but he does not answer (v.14). We have seen that this idea of a lawsuit against God's treatment of him and God's refusal to appear in court is the pivot of the first nineteen chapters. Secondly, that God's treatment of Job is characteristic of his treatment of mankind in general, for he "does not take the least notice of wickedness" (35:15). This is an excellent understanding of Job's second line of argument in chapters 21–24.

On the other hand, Elihu is also furious with the three friends for their inability to refute Job's reasonings: "Not one of you has proved Job wrong; none of you has answered his arguments" (32:12). Clearly their arguments are useless. He probably saw them as worn out clichés, so he intends to confront Job with a new set of proofs (32:14).

Ancient Jewish commentators have little good to say about Elihu. In the *Testament of Job* we read: "Elihu, inspired by Satan, spoke out...the one who spoke in him was not a human but a beast.... Elihu, Elihu, the only evil one, he had the poison of asps in his tongue." Perhaps this is too strong. Nevertheless, most modern commentators agree with the rabbis and dismiss Elihu's speeches. It is most important to notice that if his speeches had been omitted, we would not have missed them at all. True, whilst Job is to offer sacrifices to atone for the sins of his friends in the last chapter, no such instructions are given in Elihu's case. This is felt by some to justify his speeches as approved by the Lord. However, there is a total silence by Job, the friends and by the Lord, after Elihu has got through with his speeches. Does this not suggest that he was not worth replying to?

Why Reject Elihu?

- ◆ **His arrogance.** He seems to have frayed nerves, four times referring to his anger at the debate. See especially 36:4, which can be translated, *"You see before you an enlightened man"!* (Jerusalem Bible). There seem to be indications of attempts to interrupt his flow, but Elihu has no intention of giving ground to others, even though he had assured Job that should he wish to answer any point, he had only to indicate as much (33:32).

♦ **His long-windedness.** *"I am full of words"* (32:18). This is the one statement with which every reader will agree. His speeches were uninvited, yet occupy six long chapters. Job's longest speech covers four pages, as does the Lord's. Anderson calls it "rigmarole" and "bombast".

♦ **His pretensions to divine inspiration** (33:4). Had his speech been of a high calibre, with good insights, we might have been tempted to accept his claim, but this is not so. In the light of the contents of his speech, this claim is as shallow as his friends' claim to Wisdom.

♦ **His content.** In spite of his intention to refute Job with new arguments, his basic position is very little different from that of the friends. The only thing he adds which shows a development on their thought is that *suffering is disciplinary* (36:8-12). Yet compare Eliphaz at 5:17. In Elihu's eyes God metes out blessing to the righteous, and punishment to the godless (34:11, 25f).

♦ **His brutal treatment of Job.** His anger with the friends is because of their failure to bring home to Job his error.
33:8-12: Job's protestations of innocence are wrong (34:5-8), and are an evidence of his evil life.
34:5-9: Job is an evil man. He quotes Job out of context here.
34:36f.: Elihu is convinced that Job is suffering because of his sin. His protestations of innocence only add rebellion to sin.

36:17: Job is receiving the judgment due to the wicked.

36:2f.: Like the other friends Elihu is too busy playing God's advocate to listen to Job's suffering.

36:23: With all his self-assurance, Elihu had ended up very much where the friends did and with even less result. He flounders and lurches out into a windy discourse on the divine power displayed in the weather (ch. 37), which seems to add little or nothing to his argument.

A look at some elements of Elihu's argument

We do not intend to work through Elihu's argument in the way that we have with the other disputants. To do so would be tedious. Instead I will give just a broad sweep of his strengths and weaknesses.

What positive contribution does Elihu make to the arguments? First, there is his analysis of divine revelation. Job has said that the heavens are brass, that God refuses to speak to him. Elihu is scandalised by this (33:13). God, he says, constantly speaks to us, and he suggests certain ways in which this happens (33:14-19). First, there are dreams and visions; then there is the voice of conscience deep down inside each person; and finally there is physical pain, sufficient to reduce a person to complete bed rest. Now, a Christian will probably identify with all these, but, like so much in the friends' arguments, they miss the point. Job needs, not a generalised statement, but a particular word to his personal problem.

Secondly Elihu has a more developed doctrine of sickness and pain as purifying. Neither Job nor his friends had explored this theme. True, Job did make passing reference in a brilliant statement which has often been a comfort to his readers: "He knows the way that I take; when he has tested me, I shall come forth as gold" (23:10). Superb as this statement is, Job nowhere crystallises the notion, so that we must see it in his thought as a passing hint rather than a developed idea.

Thirdly, Elihu has a high concept of divine power. God is above the ways of man, so that the only thing man can do is to submit. As we have seen, his discourses end with an extensive rave about the majesty of God as seen in the weather!

However, there is so much Elihu says that is unsatisfactory. A startling example of this is his argument in favour of angelic mediators. Eliphaz had rejected this possibility in his very first speech (5:1). Job himself had expressed a desire that he might find a being to mediate in his case against God: "If only there were someone to arbitrate between us, to lay his hand upon us both" (9:33). But Job quickly repudiated any such notion. Between himself and God there could not be a mediator, human, angelic, or divine, except God himself.

Elihu has no such scruple. An angelic mediator (33:23-26) would even be able to offer a ransom for the sinner, which would find favour with God, and transform the sinner's sadness to shouts of joy. However, the one condition for the intervention of this angelic mediator is that the accused agree to confess his guilt (33:27). Which is precisely what the friends had argued all along! Elihu's idea sounds very similar to the Roman Catholic doctrine of the mediation of the saints on our behalf.

Elihu also has a view of divine justice which one must describe as inflexible: "It is unthinkable that God would do wrong, that the Almighty would pervert justice" (34:10-12). Like the friends he is shocked by Job's questioning of divine justice. To Elihu divine justice is the backbone of the universe, and to question it in any way is to destroy every possibility of right and wrong.

The consequence of this is to affirm that the apparent silence of God is due to human sin, nothing else (35:9-15). Job had complained of the silence of God, that the heavens are brass; and however he might cry in the bitterness of his soul, God was implacably silent. Elihu's answer to that is to affirm that this is entirely Job's own fault: "He does not answer when men cry out because of the arrogance of the wicked." That Job should challenge God's silence is "empty talk".

Like the friends, Elihu's main problem is that he is determined to act in God's defence, to get him off the hook:

"there is more to be said on God's behalf" (36:1), and he is determined to say it. Indeed, one might say that the whole of Elihu's bombast is designed to protect God against Job's accusations.

So it is not surprising that the climax of Elihu's case is that all human suffering, of whatever type or description, is due entirely to human sin: "if men are bound in chains, held fast by cords of affliction, he tells them what they have done – that they have sinned arrogantly" (36:7-12). His case here is not built on the corporate sin of mankind, but rather on personal, individual sin. God deals with each case on its merit, handing out blessing to the righteous and disaster to sinners. The only way the sinner can escape from this is by repentance, the one true way to happiness.

It follows that Elihu's remedy for Job's situation is repentance. Indeed, all this time God has been wooing him through suffering, "He is wooing you from the jaws of distress to a spacious place free from restriction" (36:16-17). Let Job face up to the fact that "Now (in the present time) you are laden with the judgment due to the wicked; judgment and justice have taken hold of you." So we see that this pompous young man has ended up identifying himself with the position of the three friends, and he must surely be included in the condemnation accorded to them in the conclusion: "You have not spoken of me what is right, as my servant Job has" (42:7).

Christian Reflections

33:14: "For God does speak – now one way, now another – though man may not perceive it." Elihu's picture of divine revelation is a very limited one. It basically appeals to revelation through dreams and chastisement in suffering. The Christian sees divine revelation as perhaps at times using these channels, but in no way limited to them and of being infinitely superior to them. He reveals himself to us through the written word, which in itself contains the revelation of the living Word, Jesus Christ.

It is as we reflect on Jesus Christ that we are by revelation being transformed into becoming a pale reflection of him (2 Cor. 3:18. See also Heb. 1:2).

Do you think Elihu's arguments in favour of divine revelation through dreams and pain is valid? Give biblical and/or personal experiences. Are they adequate? In what way do you experience God's revelation, in general, and to yourself in particular?

36:8-12: "If men are bound in chains...he tells them what they have done – that they have sinned arrogantly." We have said that Elihu has a more developed idea of suffering as being curative. However, this needs to be clarified. Unfortunately his concept of the way in which God gives and uses suffering is essentially punitive, well illustrated in this passage. Christian understanding of God and suffering is educational and curative, as Job himself had very briefly suggested (23:10). Peter echoes Job's thought when he declares: "These (griefs and trials) have come so that your faith – of greater worth than gold, which perishes even though refined by fire – may be proved genuine" (1 Pet.1:6-7. See also Rom. 5:3-5 and 2 Cor. 12:7-10).

These three passages give a very clear idea of the great value of suffering in the hand of God. How do they help you to understand your own suffering? We ALL suffer in some form or other. Verbalise your suffering and ask yourself what light these passages throw on them.

33:33 and 35:16: "Listen to me, be silent, and I will teach you wisdom... Job opens his mouth with empty talk." Elihu's speech is a massive put-down to Job and his friends, and, one fears, a massive inflation of his own pride. This is a pity, since in his opening words (ch.32) we have a feeling of sympathy with the frustrations of this young man. He has listened in to the learned debates of older men and has been driven to despair, so that he cannot contain himself. Yet what he actually says, in a long non-ending speech, contributes little or nothing to clarifying matters.

He is, in fact, not unlike young men (and women) today. The rationalisations of older people, their traditionalism, their

closed circles, dogmatism on minor issues, drive young people
to rebellion. As such, young people need to be listened to, and
above all sympathised with. When, however, they come to
actually saying or doing something, it is seldom original, and
not infrequently repeats the same errors of older people. This is
so vividly portrayed in young Elihu. In striking contrast the
apostles of Jesus were young spiritual roughnecks, whose one
ambition was not to spend time in endless discussion of difficult
questions, but to preach the gospel.
Reflect on these observations within your own circles.

27. The Lord's Answer to Job – Chapters 38–41
Answer or Diversion?

We have waited with baited breath for God's reply to Job. That
God must reply is certain because on the one hand the book
would be incomplete, but also because Job has challenged God
on several points as to his justice. If God does not speak now
Job will have left him speechless! Also, the four friends, in
their failure to convince Job of God's justice in inflicting him
with these evils, have put God's prestige at stake.

What shall we make of God's answer?
Chapters 38–41 leave many readers confused. What do the rain
and the ice (38:28-30), the stupidity of the ostrich (39:13-15),
the hippo, and the crocodile (40:15-24) have to do with such
profound questions as, "Why do the innocent suffer?", "Is there
disinterested piety?" "How can a man be right before God?" Or
the tragedy which is so characteristic of life?
    Some readers react negatively. "A magnificent impertinence"
(J.C.Ball). To Carl Jung, Job's God was a bully. He did not
answer Job's heart-searching questions, he blustered. "Like
shaking a rattle at a crying child in order to divert its attention
from its hunger pangs" (R.A. McKenzie). It is as though God
said, "Job, look at the magnificence of my universe, and forget

about your little worries!" Some complain of the disappearance of ethics into entertainment. Job, the hero of the story, has called God's bluff, and all God can do is waffle! (Berniéres)

However, in the narrator's eyes the real hero is God. Indeed, according to the story-teller, God is the real hero in Job's eyes as well, for he ends confessing his inability to understand and submitting himself to God's infinitely superior wisdom and justice. What is more, the rabbis of Judaism, whilst questioning the divine explanation and meaning of books like Proverbs, never questioned the divine origin of this book. The Christian church has also always accepted the divine inspiration of this book. Thus neither Job, nor the narrator, nor the rabbis, nor the church see Job as wrong-footing God. Rather, Job is an example of true piety (James 5:11).

A question of expectations. A reader's judgment depends on their expectation of what will happen when God intervenes. What is Job expecting? A declaration of his own innocence! What are his friends expecting? A thunderbolt to destroy the renegade who had shaken their little world! The important thing to take stock of is that we are all expecting something when the Lord finally speaks.

What do *you* expect? An intellectual response to the problem of innocent suffering? A justification of God's ways with man? Sympathy and compassion for the bruised sufferer? Perhaps our frustration lies in the fact that we don't hear in God's discourse what we are predisposed to hear, but then perhaps we are not listening to God. It is probable that the reader's reaction will tell more about the reader than about Job or his God!

God's answer

In reality God does not answer Job or any other of the debaters. Why should he? It is not for God to enter into the fracas and lash out against the disputants. He speaks, but he speaks as God, the Creator of the universe, about the mystery of the cosmos. This is as it should be, for he has no need to defend himself!

Box 23 – God's Answer to Job.
As we approach the end of the book we feel that God *must* reply to Job. We had expected his reply after chapter 31, but the narrator has kept us in awful suspense. Now we are fired up to hear his answer.

Yet here we might well feel disappointed. God apparently spends his time with what someone has called "a carnival of animals". God takes Job by the hand and, instead of answering his questionings, treats him to a tour of the universe. He sees the magnificence of the earth, the pounding of the oceans, the weather patterns hurtling over the surface of the earth, the constellations, the incredible variety of the animal kingdom, much of which is unintelligible to man, and the whole is concluded by two half-real, half-mythological creatures, Behemoth and Leviathan.

The reader may well scratch his head and wonder what all this has to do with the heart-rending questions which the book has raised: Will a good man deny the Lord under stress? Why do innocent people suffer? Is there really justice in the order of the world? Does God mete out justice in perfect fairness, punishing bad people, and making good people endlessly happy?

Since the Lord's speech is the capstone of the book, we shall expect some kind of response to those profound questions, but like the teaching of Jesus, the answer is far from being a direct "yes" or "no". Rather the answers are given in a roundabout way. This serves the purpose of making the reader think through what is said carefully and prayerfully. Only thus will the Lord's speech respond to our questionings.

In chapter 9 we noted that if God did speak, "He (Job) would be barraged by a thousand questions, a thousand assertions, a thousand proofs, none of which he could answer." And this is precisely what happens. God's answer ranges over a whole cosmic panorama – earth and sea, the dawn, meteors, constellations, wild animals, and prolonged descriptions of Behemoth and Leviathan, two half-real, half-fantastic creatures. We are offered a tour of the universe with God as our guide! Is this all no more than a magnificent diversion from the real questions which plague the book? But, but, but – God in the Bible seldom offers direct answers. He says things in a round-about sort of way, which drives us to hard thinking. Only thus can his truth become our truth!

Two observations will be helpful here:

1. *Job passed the test*. The accusation of Satan (ch. 1) was that Job's piety was not sincere, that it was self-motivated. Remove the blessings and Job will curse you. Whatever else he did, Job did not curse God – ever. But also, how does God's answer relate to Job, the friends, and to their contentions? This is fundamentally important. Job's friends' accusation was that he had sinned grievously and merited punishment. In his answer the Lord is totally silent on this issue. By remaining silent God recognises the validity of Job's protestations of innocence and the falseness of his friends' imputations. So Job is vindicated. That the narrator wants us to understand this is finally assured in the full restoration of Job in the last chapter, and the Lord's command to the friends to ask Job to intercede on their behalf: "Because you have not spoken well of me, as my servant Job has" (42:7).

Throughout the book Job has shown himself to be a true believer, one might say, an incredible believer. The cards have been stacked against him. He has been desolated, deprived and vilified, yet he has clung tenaciously to a belief in the goodness of God. He has broken through to new depths and heights of the goodness of God, whilst confessing his continued bewilderment at the way the universe is run. It is no cheap and easy believism, but a rugged, painful, experience-oriented trust in the essential goodness of a God who has apparently demolished his life and hope. This is faith of the highest order.

2. *God met Job's felt needs*. Rather than answer his questions, God directs his answers to Job's *needs*, which fortunately coincided with his deepest desires. It is probably true to say that when we are reduced to nothing, we begin to get our priorities right! What then were Job's true needs and desires?

He desired to meet God. The silence of heaven had increased Job's agony tenfold. Now God speaks, and he speaks exclusively to Job (38:1; 40:6). This was no mere voice of conscience, but a visible manifestation of divine power (cp. Exod. 19:16; Ezek. 1:4). Job's basic need, and by now his burning desire, was not for a simple explanation of his sufferings (this was not offered to him!) but a personal encounter with the living God, and this was graciously conceded by God. *There could be no greater privilege!* Compare 42:5: "My ears had heard of you (=religion, secondary knowledge, hearsay), but now my eyes have seen you."

But there is something else here which we might let slip by unnoticed. It is that God meets him no longer as the Almighty, but as 'the LORD'. Read again Box 6, where we noted that striking change of names for God. In the first two chapters he is 'the LORD', but throughout the debate which follows, right up to this point, God is the Almighty – distant, austere, seemingly indifferent to Job's cries. Now, when God appears he does so as the Lord, the gracious, unsparingly generous God with whom Job had walked in intimate fellowship through life. So God's speech must be seen as the reappearance of one who wishes to shower Job with blessing and grace.

Then, **Job desired respite from his sufferings** (10:20: "Are not my few days almost over? Turn away from me so I can have a moment's joy"). His cosmic tour under God's guidance is a respite from pain rather than occasion for happiness. When we suffer disaster, or pain, the whole world comes crashing down. *Why me?* This is because the world revolves around us and our concerns. God is helping Job get things in perspective.

Our suffering is not the earth's centre of gravity, it is a tiny part (though to us a very important part) of the incredible mosaic of the whole.

But why the cosmic tour? It is essential to understand the *humour* in these chapters. Very much depends on what we bring to our reading of them. If we ourselves bring hostility and disharmony, that is what we shall read into them. However, I believe there is a gentle irony in God's voice. We sense an understanding firmness which reminds us of a father. There is a world of difference in a father's tone between *"You stupid little boy"* and *"You funny little boy"*. Is it possible to see the Lord's eyes twinkling as he tweaks Job's ear? If we miss this humour, if we read hostility into God's words, we shall miss the real point of these chapters.

If, for example, we read the following sentences as sarcasm, they are extremely hurtful: "Surely *you* know, for *you* were already born [at creation]! *You* have lived so many years!" (38:21), or, "Does the hawk take flight by *your* wisdom.... Does the eagle soar at *your* command?" (39:26-27). In that case we would be right to condemn God, but read as gentle irony they become tender humour. And there is more healing in gentle humour than in learned discourses on the meaning of suffering!

Job is reproached
Yet Job *is* being reproached (38:1,2; 40:2), and he knew it (40:4,5). These two sections into which the Lord's speech is divided are both designed to scold Job, and we prefer the word 'scold' to any other. On what grounds is Job being scolded?

Firstly, *for criticising God's ways without understanding them.* "Who are you to question my wisdom with your ignorant, empty words?" (38:2, Good News Bible). God reproaches Job for throwing up a volley of vain words about a subject he cannot possibly fathom in all its length and breadth. Old peanut brain has thought to question God's ways. Job thinks he could have made a better job of running the universe! He seems unaware of the fact that he is viewing the world and reality from a worm's eye view. In chapters 38 and 39 God invites him to a bird's eye view, or rather a divine eye view of the universe, responding to his mentality by showing him how utterly narrow and confined is his world view, how insignificant he is as a being. There is no way he can understand even a fragmentary part of God's activity in the universe. The wild animals, the weather, the constellations, are all observable wonders, but man is incapable of understanding them (much more so in Job's days). They are equally part of God's all-wise creation. That this rebuke stung Job very deeply is evident from his determination to *"put a hand over my mouth"* (40:4). In passing it is well to note that Job himself had earlier admitted that God's ways pass man's ability to comprehend (21:22).

Secondly, Job is guilty of *discrediting God's justice* (40:8a). We saw that, after finding his personal vindication in chapter 19, Job proceeded to question God's justice in the world. Job argued that we live in a world which doesn't seem to be governed on any moral principles at all (chs. 21 and 24). In this Job was grossly wrong and was guilty of denying God's justice. Job (and we) know so very little of the principles involved in moral judgment.

In response, in a brilliant satire, biting but not cruel, the Lord invites Job to take over the reins of the world (40:9-14), to appear in it as God, and to annihilate the wicked. Would this be the solution? Would it be a victory for truth and righteousness? In effect God says, "You play at being God for an hour! Then I myself will stand by in wondering amazement" (v.14).

Finally, Job is censured *for condemning God in order to justify himself* (40:8b). Job has proposed taking God to court. He agrees with his friends that God is responsible for his sufferings. The friends argue that this is evidence of his personal sin. Job argues that it is evidence of God's displeasure and therefore of his *injustice!* "I've been wronged!" he screams.

In his second phase (chs. 21 and 24), Job extends his accusation of injustice to God's rule of the world as a whole. Psalm 58 sets out the desire of ancient Israelites for a display of

Box 24 – A satire, tender as a mother's kiss.

There have been many negative reactions to the Lord's speech by commentators. Carl Jung accused him of bullying. Unable to confront Job's piercing questions, God tries to divert attention to things which appear more trivial, like shaking a rattle at a crying child in order to divert its attention from its hunger.

However, I think it depends very much on two things. First, the reader's expectation of what God will say when he does speak. Job's friends will have expected a bolt of lightning to destroy the blasphemer. Job will have expected a justification of his cause. In the event, God does neither.

The second thing is that it very much depends on the tones in which we hear the voice of God. If we read it as harsh, we shall hear God ridiculing Job and his suffering, and we shall rightly be angry with God. In that case we may be learning more about the reader than about Job's story and our narrator's intention. If in contrast we read God's speech as gentle irony, our understanding of what is happening will be enlightened. It was Dr. G Campbell Morgan who described the Lord's speech as "A satire, tender as a mother's kiss". Read like this the speech becomes pure goodness and gentleness.

God's retributive justice. Of the wicked the psalmist cries, "Break the teeth in their mouths, O God...let them vanish like water that flows away...like the slug melting away as it moves ....The righteous will be glad when they are avenged, when they bathe their feet in the blood of the wicked. Then [and one might add, only then] men will say, 'Surely the righteous still are rewarded; surely there is a God who judges the earth'." We want to see, before our very eyes, the punishment of those we consider evil.

But what would really be achieved with such a rigid rule of righteous judgment? A Peruvian friend of mine, Dr. Samuel Escobar, wrote a booklet entitled: "I don't agree with God." In it he complains of the words of Jesus: "Love your enemies...that you may be sons of your Father in heaven. He causes his sun to rise on the evil and the good, and sends rain on the righteous and the unrighteous" (Matt. 5:44-45). If I were God, he argues, I would ensure that the violators of my law never saw the face of the sun and their lands would be parched and fruitless. However, as he reflects on what this entails he is led to ask, Which one of us is truly righteous, which one of us would want God to act in this way to us personally? Thank God he doesn't! In another place the psalmist cries: "O LORD, hear my prayer, listen to my cry for mercy.... Do not bring your servant into judgment, for no-one living is righteous before you" (Ps. 143:1-2). By such a measure we should be eternally grateful to God that he does not deal with any of us on the strict basis of our personal deserving, punishment or reward.

Job has wanted to take God to court. But this is dangerous territory! When I take someone to court it is because of my sense of outrage, of injustice, in which I am the innocent party. My innocence depends on my belief that the other party is guilty, damnably guilty. I go to court in order to obtain a confession and damages from my opponent. He must be condemned, so that I may be acquitted. Since Job knows himself to be innocent, to be the victim of a gross injustice, he is certain of God's guilt!

Whose court is it, anyway? We have seen that for Job there is a conflict of thought. At times it seems he wants to impeach God in a court he has convoked. Mostly it is God's court and he is the prosecutor, judge and jury. But because he is convinced of his innocence, Job is certain that he will be vindicated, even in God's case against him. There is another aspect to the courtroom scenes. One of the primary functions of ancient courts was to seek reconciliation for the aggrieved party. So often bitterness is due to misunderstanding. If dialogue can be established and explanations made, very often the grievance disappears. What Job wanted was vindication in his lawsuit. What the Lord offers him is reconciliation.

Yet it is a reconciliation which can only be effected by facing Job up to the errors of his own thought and talk, whilst recognising the basic validity of his claim to innocence. That is a delicate task, which must neither inflate Job's ego, nor give the impression his friends are right in their accusations. It is done in a brilliant satire, worthy of divinity!

As the man who dares to accuse God, Job is invited to step forward (40:2), not to be punished, but to be invited to play God's role, to "adorn yourself with glory and splendour,...clothe yourself in honour and majesty" (v.10). Glory, splendour, honour and majesty are only attributable to God. As God, Job can take over the role of chief administrator of justice in the universe: "Unleash the fury of your wrath, look at every proud man and bring him low...crush the wicked," etc. (vv.11,12); while God will look on in admiration! (v.14). One can feel Job cringing at the stupidity of his own position.

> He is righteous before God. He is rich. His heart is full of righteousness, since it seems to him that God is doing his work badly, and he thinks that he himself is righteous, and if you were to allow him to steer the ship, he would wreck it. He wants to oust God from the control of the world, and himself take the helm of creation, allotting sorrows and joys, punishments and rewards, to all. Poor man (Augustine of Hippo).

Christian Reflections

38:2: "Who is this that darkens my counsel with words without knowledge?" One of the major emphases of this book is its attack on human ignorance, especially the ignorance of those who consider themselves to be wise! This was true of the three friends, of young Elihu, and of Job himself. Job's book suggests an

ongoing conflict among the "wise" men. The writer of
Ecclesiastes slammed the arrogance of the wise men, and
questioned whether they were not fooling themselves (8:16-17).
"No one can comprehend," he says, "what goes on under the
sun." That might well serve as the essence of the Lord's
invitation to Job in these chapters.

Both Old and New Testaments recognise the limitations of
our knowledge. Read Deuteronomy 29:29, which indicates that
God himself has put serious limitations on our ability to
understand. He has revealed much, but he has also hidden much,
that we might learn humility in our search for truth. Paul sums
up our present state of knowledge: "Now [at the present time]we
see but a poor reflection as in a mirror." Mirrors in those days
were polished bronze disks, which gave a very limited reflection

---

Box 25 – God takes up Job's gauntlet.
This is the heart of the LORD's response to Job. Job has
sought to put God in the dock, charged with the crime of
flaunting the law of retribution. A good life has not been
rewarded with blessing, and evil men are getting away
with their crimes. The law of retribution has collapsed.
Job, having been given a clear picture of a universe
bountifully created on the basis of grace, is now invited
to press his case (v.2). This he declines to do (vv.3-5),
conscious that he is in the wrong.

The LORD, and it is 'the LORD' (see Box 6), who has
graciously walked with him through his former decades
of happiness, who now confronts him (vv.6-14). There is
a brilliant humour in these words. Job is invited by God
to take over the reins of the universe, to have a go at being
God. He can 'Unleash the fury of your wrath... crush the
wicked...' and mete out justice on every evil man. God
will stand by in awe at the might and wisdom of Job.

It is essential to read these words not in a cruel, satirical
tone, but with the gentleness of a mother chuckling at the
foolish antics of her bad-tempered child.

of reality. Even the word "reflection" here is a word which we know, "enigma". What a frail limitation of our knowledge this implies! Perhaps the best thing is to meditate on the words of Paul in Romans 11:33-36: "Oh the depth of the riches of the wisdom and knowledge of God! How unsearchable his judgments, and his paths beyond tracing out!...to him be the glory for ever."

Reflect on the words of Paul in the passage indicated.

39:9: "Who let the wild donkey go free?" What a superb picture of God's creative and caring presence in the animal kingdom this passage portrays! Lions, goats, fawns, wild ox, the ostrich, the horse, the hawk, the eagle, crowd our canvas. Add to this his concern for the ridiculous-looking hippo in 40:15, who "was made along with you [Job]", and "ranks first among the works of God". While there is a strong note of humour in this, we are taught to appreciate and be concerned for all God's creation. The New Testament affirms that all creation is derived from the creative genius of Jesus Christ, the Son of God: "Through him all things were made; without him nothing was made that has been made" (John 1:3, cp. Heb 1:2; Col. 1:16; 1 Cor. 8:6). It must be remembered that the biblical concept of creation is that it is not a simple, one-off event, but an ongoing process, so that even today we can contain in our worldview the concept of Jesus as the ongoing Creator of every living thing! To him be the glory!

How might this idea of Jesus as the creator transform your manner of dealing with physical creation whether in plant, in animal or bird, and in human beings?

Behemoth and Leviathan

Incredibly the Lord's speech is further prolonged by a description of two weird and wonderful creatures, Behemoth (40:15-24) and Leviathan (ch. 41). Though their description is poetic and far surpasses the original model, they have strikingly similar characteristics with the hippopotamus and the crocodile.

Box 26 – Retribution or Grace?
At this point we reach the climax of the Lord's answer to
Job, but what an incredible answer it is. We are introduced
to two weird creatures, Behemoth (40:15) and Leviathan
(41:1). As we read their amazing description we wonder
whether they were ever real, or whether they are really
mythical. They may be the hippopotamus and the crocodile, yet their description seems to suggest that they are
dressed up, half-imaginary versions of these two animals.

Why are they introduced at all? Like chapters 38 and
39, they are clearly God's way of showing Job that the
universe is not run on logical grounds of rewards and
punishment. Rather the universe is permeated by grace,
by the mind of a God who delights in every creature he
has made, down to the most insignificant, the seemingly
stupid, and even the weird.

Retribution, so narrowly defined by Job and his friends,
succeeds in imposing strict limitations on God's actions.
He is simply and solely the guardian of a strict moral
order. By contrast grace is free, unrestricted, and creative
love. It is the heart of the Creator, with whom Job and his
friends, and we ourselves, have to do. We may not
understand all his ways but we must learn to run free in
the fields of God's love, and if it takes a tour of the
universe, with the climaxing view of two weird and
wonderful creatures, to achieve this picture of God's free
and creative love, then so be it.

Behemoth the Hippo – read 40:15-24
Startlingly, the creation of the hippo is closely linked to the
creation of man, of Job in particular (v.15). "This weird animal,"
says God, "is as much an integral and important part of my
creation as you are." Second only in size to the elephant, this

"river horse", as his name means, appears to us as a fairly useless brute, a great lump of walking blubber. You would expect it to be a tough meat-eater, but it eats grass like a cow. It looks like rippling muscle (vv.17-18), yet it is useless for work, totally untamable (v.24), preferring instead to spend most of his time lying among the lotus plants, "hidden among the reeds in the marsh" (v.21). Its huge body size, weighing up to three tons, set on comically short legs, its absurd protruding eyes and nostrils, all contribute to making us think it the most ridiculous of animals.

So what is the point of Behemoth? Clearly he is all part of the satire of the Lord's response. Here is this bizarre creature, useless to man and beast alike, yet he is placed alongside man in God's creative activity. Indeed, "He ranks first among the works of God" (v.19). This big, grotesque, worthless, dim-witted animal is a special part of God's plans, and the object of his care. Here indeed is a picture of divine grace. That we cannot *understand* why God created such a being is irrelevant.

Leviathan the Crocodile – read chapter 41
The crocodile stands in startling contrast with the hippo. If the hippo is a picture of the absurd in God's creation, the crocodile is a picture of the devilish. He is a fierce, vicious, meat-eating savage. Again and again the Lord emphasises his brutality and the futility of man trying to tame him: "Can you put a hook through his nose?... Can you make a pet of him?... Will traders barter for him?... Any hope of subduing him is false". The fatality of those who try to tame him is sure: "If you lay a hand on him, you will remember the struggle and never do it again!" (v.8).

The crocodile of the Nile lives up to forty years, grows up to six metres in length and weighs a ton. It feeds on antelope, deer, and horse, which venture to the water, and is known to attack humans viciously.

Now, we must remember that Job was a man of the desert. He gives no indication of having been a well-travelled man, so it is virtually certain that he had never seen a crocodile. In the desert there is plenty of time for talk, and stories of the crocodile of the Nile will have been numerous, always, of course, over-exaggerated. The Lord plays on this descriptive overkill, treating Job to a carnivalesque description of this monster in a riot of detail! Clearly Job is being introduced to the supreme model of evil, and, says God, in effect, he is not outside of my control.

The naming of the monster crocodile as **Leviathan** is important. Leviathan appears several times in the Old Testament, often in Job. Leviathan is a picture myth widely spread over the ancient world, and the recall of that name, with all its emotional associations, will have been a spine-chiller to Job. Notice that our 'croc' beast is clearly not a crocodile! Rather he is a dragon patterned on the form of the crocodile. Out of every point of his head he spits fire (vv.18-21). An array of words are used to express this: flashes, firebrands, sparks of fire, smoke – pour from his eyes, his mouth, his nostrils, his breath.

In the ancient mythology of Job's world Leviathan was a sea monster who fought with the gods in the creation of the world. He had to be overcome in order that the world might be created, yet he lingers on as the sum of all evil within the world. In other parts of our book Job himself has made reference to this monster. In chapter 3, in his very first speech, Job refers to the professional mourners at a funeral who curse death, thus "arousing Leviathan" (3:8). In chapter 7 he asks God, "Am I...the monster of the deep, that you put me under guard?" (7:12). In chapter 9, in a passage which celebrates God's awesome power, Job asserts, "God does not restrain his anger; even the cohorts of Rahab cowered at his feet" (9:13). Leviathan, the sea monster, and Rahab are both the apex of evil, of everything that threatens man's existence, in ancient thought.

Now it must be clear that the book, and the conclusion of God's speech, cannot be ending on a damp squib, as though God were saying, look at that funny creature the crocodile! No, this hideous Leviathan points to the origin and essence of evil – of the evil Job himself has savoured – to the Satan who dominates the first two chapters of the book. In effect God says to Job: "This evil being who has sought to destroy you is under my control, and eventually will be destroyed." So, in the opening chapters, though Satan wants to destroy Job, he cannot touch a hair of Job's head without divine permission, and in some way Satan will only be achieving something that God wants to achieve.

Since Leviathan is the exemplar of venom, he leaves open the question as to the origin of evil. Here is this hideously foul and vicious creature, which is seemingly godlike – the Satan – who chapters 1 and 2 indicate had been the agent of Job's destruction. Yet he is being used to achieve God's purposes. He has a length of rope in the short term, but in the long run he is heavily chained.

But why then has Job suffered such awful disaster? Is there some purpose in evil? We shudder to think there might be an affirmative answer to this question. Yet it would be simplistic to deny it. There is an element of contingency in all evil. We are all affected by it, and it affects all our life and temperament.

In this case there will very often be the question as to the lesser or greater evil. Moral decisions have to be made based on the lesser evil, as much as on the greater good. In Job's case God might well have left Job in the condition in which we found him at the beginning of the book, rich and prosperous, just and good, generous and kind, yet tending toward complacency, self-indulgence, pride. God wants something far more wonderful than Job could ever imagine, though on just one occasion he broke through to discover a thread of good in his sufferings: "when he has tested me, I shall come forth as gold" (23:10). Momentarily Job discovered a divine, positive, beneficial purpose in his sufferings.

There is no contingency or creature outside the command of the God who cares – only thus can we bear the pain of suffering and live with mystery. Unencumbered trust is God's goal.

Christian Reflections

40:7: "Brace yourself like a man..." Older versions gave the more literal translation: "Gird up your loins like a man." In biblical times men wore a flowing tunic which they gathered at the waist and tied with a belt or cord in order to move into action for running or hard work. It is clear that God wants no grovelling before him. He positively invites Job to serious dialogue. He esteems Job worthy and capable of such a debate with the Almighty. When Ezekiel fell down on his face in self-humbling before the Lord, he was immediately commanded to stand up (Ezek. 2:1). The same figure of speech is used often in the New Testament, though modern versions lose it by more direct modern translations (see Luke 12:35; 1 Pet. 1:13).

What kind of mental attitude ought we to have when coming to God? What does the Lord look for in our approach? Looking at these verses, what do you learn about our required state of mind?

40:8: "Would you condemn me to justify yourself?" The theme of justification – set in a courtroom – dominates this book. Job wanted justification of his conduct before God. As always the Old Testament model falls short of the New. It leaves open the question of man's ultimate standing before God, but the New Testament opens up this whole investigation. In the final analysis none of us can stand justified before God in our own merit. Paul puts it eloquently: "When the kindness and love of God our Saviour appeared, he saved us, not because of righteous things we had done, but because of his mercy" (Titus 3:5).

See also Romans 3:22, Galatians 2:15-16 and Philippians 3:7-9. What do these passages teach us about our standing before God?

40:15 and 19: "Look at the Behemoth." The hippo is one of God's object lessons. He is hideously funny, what possible purpose can there be for such a creature? God says he has a special place in his affections for the hippo. One of my favourite films was Spielberg's *ET,* of which I have a little figurine peering out on my desk from a flower pot. *ET,* the weird-looking creature from outer space, provokes negative and hostile reactions in the community, except for one little boy. Society cannot suffer such a bizarre being in its midst, and is determined to destroy it. This is a parable of human nature. We are instinctively afraid of what comes into our midst, what we don't understand. Foreigners appear as a threat to all communities. They don't speak our language, dress oddly, have different customs.

Hitler wanted to do away with everything he considered ugly and useless – Jews, gypsies, and the mentally handicapped. He wanted a pure Aryan race, to be marked by physical, social and intellectual oneness, intolerant of anything supposedly inferior. God's concern for the ridiculous hippo is God's reply to Hitler, a lesson and example to us all.

What/who might there be in your community, workplace, church, which provokes a negative reaction in you? Be honest with yourself here. How ought you to consider it/them in the light of God's Word?

41:1: "Can you pull in the leviathan with a fishhook?" No attempt is made in this book, or elsewhere in the Old Testament to identify the Satan of Job 1–2 with the serpent of Genesis 3. It is not in fact until the last book of the Bible, Revelation, that the identification of the various figures of consummate evil are blended into one: "And the great dragon was cast down, the old serpent, he that is called the Devil and Satan, the deceiver of the whole world" (Rev. 12:9). Whenever the last conflict with satanic forces of evil are mentioned in Scripture, we are driven back to the book of Revelation as the ultimate description of this battle. We may not be able to unravel all the symbolism of that book, but one driving fact stands out irrefutably – it is designed to show us that evil will be finally defeated and totally destroyed, and that that victory will be in the hands of the Rider on the White Horse, who has this name: KING OF KINGS AND LORD OF LORDS, that is, of Jesus Christ, our Lord (Rev. 19:11-21).

The final triumph of good over evil is deeply embedded in human thought. Twentieth century works like Tolkien's *Lord of the Rings* and Lewis' *Narnia* series give modern expression to this. In another way it is expressed in the words of Jesus:

"Blessed are the meek, for they will inherit the earth" (Matt. 5:5).

In what way might this divinely guaranteed triumph of good over evil be expressed in the twenty-first century? Is it just a pipe dream, when, as Job himself argued so convincingly in chapters 21 and 24, evil seems to be triumphant? What experiences within your own life and surroundings assure you of that triumph? How does the Cross of Jesus guarantee that triumph?

28. Job's complete recovery – Chapter 42

Job humbles himself – read 42:1-6

It would undoubtedly have been better to have included these verses at the end of chapter 41. All chapter divisions in our Bible are artificial, introduced hundreds of years after the original writing. They should never be considered divinely inspired. In this case the only correct place for Job's confession is immediately following on from the Lord's speech.

First, notice that Job's confession and repentance happens without the restoration spelt out in the rest of this chapter. Incredibly, he makes his peace with God with no prospects of restoration – this was never offered to him by the Lord.

The first divine speech ended (40:1-2) with a direct challenge to Job to speak up in the light of the Lord's self-revelation. Job had attempted in his speeches to contend with the Almighty, to correct him, to accuse the Lord of not managing his world with justice. The Lord has demonstrated that as the Creator of the universe, of things comprehensible and incomprehensible, he knows perfectly well what he does. Job, on the other hand, must of necessity view things from a very limited and tiny perspective. Job's response is to acknowledge his wretchedness, and express his determination to maintain silence. He recognizes that he has spoken out-of-turn and in ignorance (40:4-5).

Now, following the Lord's second speech, Job immediately

humbles himself. He begins by an affirmation that God does all things wisely, and achieves all his objectives. Job recognises that though he personally had not been able to understand what the Lord was doing with him in his suffering, there must have been a divine purpose, a plan. In other words, Job concedes that everything happening in the world takes place within the boundaries of God's purpose and wisdom.

Job then proceeds to quote two questions addressed to him in the divine speeches. First, the accusation that he has spoken with insufficient knowledge of ultimate reality (v.3 with 38:2). He humbly confesses that he had entered into areas where he was incompetent to judge, undoubtedly referring to his speeches in chapters 21 and 24, where he had blasted off against the Almighty's apparent indifference to evil and suffering in the world.

The second divine word to Job came from the Lord's second

Box 27 – Job's recovery.

Job's recovery is embraced in two phases: first, his repentance (42:1-6); then, his restoration (vv.7-17). His repentance is marked by the confession that he has spoken unwisely and ignorantly, but also by the triumphant affirmation that in the midst of his sufferings and questionings, he has finally met with God, which in reality had been the deepest need and longing of his heart (v.3). In comparison with this, all his former knowledge of God had been second-hand hearsay, now 'my eyes have seen you' (v.5).

Job's restoration is complete. He is restored in the eyes of his friends as they are ordered to request his prayers on their behalf, thus recognizing that they have all along been in the wrong. Job is thus declared innocent of their charges. He is restored in the eyes of the community which had so cruelly rejected him, by the doubling to him of everything he had ever had before.

speech (40:7), and was a demand that Job stop talking and carefully listen to what the Lord has to say. Job's speeches have been full of expressed doubts about God's ways, now it is God's turn to do the questioning, and let Job answer (v.4). However, Job is in no mood for answering now. He is conscious that everything he has said in questioning the divine justice and wisdom has been claptrap.

Job has become completely transfixed and transformed by the Lord's speeches. And here indeed Job expresses his captivated wonder. During all his previous life, a life so commendable that even God boasted about it (1:8), his religion had been one of hearsay, no doubt through the songs of his people and in the teaching of their elders and religious leaders. Now he recognises that through his sufferings and deprivations he has acquired something far more wonderful – a personal experience of God, an intimate encounter with the Lord. He has *seen* God, and that transfixing gaze had worked a transformation in his inner being.

His confession climaxes with what is in essence a confession of sin, "Therefore I despise myself and repent in dust and ashes." He confesses his failure, but his confession is the beginning of a new life.

Christian Reflections

42:5: "My ears heard of you..." Job confesses to having lived on borrowed faith. God has no grandchildren. Natural religion is a barrier to fellowship with God because it is based purely on tradition and second-hand knowledge, and often leads to fear, religious slavery and even bigotry.

Do you live your faith by hearsay? Do you see God? (Cp. 19:25. See 2 Cor. 3:18 – to see is to be transformed!)

Verse 6: "I despise myself and repent in dust and ashes." What a long, long way Job has come before he finally blurts out these words. Perhaps that is true of most of us; it takes a long time,

and costs a lot of self-humbling to get there. Yet it is the essence
of the message of Jesus for the whole of mankind: "The kingdom
of God is near. Repent and believe the good news!" Confession
is good for the soul, but true confession, being brutally honest
with oneself, is hard to face up to.

**Try measuring yourself by self-words to calculate the
nature of your on-going repentance before God. There are
many self-words in English, some negative, e.g. self-seeking,
self-conceit, self-pity, etc.; some positive, e.g. self-assurance,
self-respect, self-fulfilment; yet others are neutral, self-
portrait. Perhaps it is by measuring oneself against these
that we can come to know and evaluate ourselves better.
Build up a list of "self-" words, negative and positive. How
do you measure up to them?**

"They Lived Happily Ever After" – read 42:7-17
This "happy ending" to the book of Job has caused irritation to
some readers. Verses 1-6 seem like a fitting climax to the whole
story, Job humbling himself before the Lord, receiving a vision
of God which would burn into his soul and transform his whole
thinking, his whole life. And there, they think, would have been
a suitable ending point. Whereas, the account of Job's restoration
has about it something of a fairy story quality. Is it, perhaps, a
little too unreal?

Restoration in the eyes of his friends – read 42:7-9
The book has been dominated by a lengthy argument between
Job and his friends, in which they have persistently accused
him of being a wicked man who was justly suffering merited
punishment from God. In his speeches (chs. 38–41), God never
so much as touches on their accusations, which in itself was a
justification of Job.

But now God states it very clearly. Three times he refers to
Job as "my servant Job", which rams the fact down the friends'
throat. They had counted themselves as true servants of God as
they levelled their accusations against Job. Now the Lord places

himself firmly on the side of Job. It is not difficult for us to imagine the self-humbling of these three proud men. They had been so absolutely sure that they were in the right. Not once did they leave any space for the thought that perhaps Job had some element of truth in what he claimed – his own innocence.

The Lord makes patently clear his disgust with the way they have conducted their vendetta against our hero: "I am angry with you...", and he makes it crystal clear that it was the content of their arguments which provoke his divine anger: "because you have not spoken of me what is right, as my servant Job has."

They are ordered to show their repentance by coming, cap in hand, to Job, in a repentant attitude, and to ask for his forgiveness. Job's response was immediately gracious. He had been justifiably angry with his friends, but he refuses to entertain any bitterness. He doubled his knees and prayed for them! He recognised that grace had intervened, that God had entered the inmost shrine of their thinking, and turned it round. Only grace can make a proud, arrogant man, solidly supported in his arguments by two like-minded friends, confess that he has been wrong all along. Job undoubtedly recognised this and prayed for them.

Restoration in the eyes of his community – read 42:10-17
Job appeared in the eyes of his former community as a dirty old beggar. They had driven him out of their town, away from the dwellings of men. Above everything else in biblical times, his rotting social status, his rotting body, were in the eyes of men a sure token of God's wrath upon him.

Why the rubbish heap? Probably nowhere else for him to go. To the east lay the horrific Judean desert, where he would have quickly died of hunger. To the north and south lay scrub land, where the shepherds herded their sheep, and where they would have driven the beggar off with stones. To the west lay the fields of the people, where any person finding him on their property would have driven him off. The rubbish mound was the only place left for him. There he could at least scavenge some food, and perhaps sitting there, looking at his beloved town, which had been the heart of his past joys, he could still cling to the possibility of a return to it, or at least be buried within its boundary.

But they had not left him alone on his garbage tip. The drunkards had sung coarse songs ridiculing him in their taverns, they told jokes about him (30:9). They jeered at him as they walked by the rubbish heap (30:1); the scum of society spat in his face if they had occasion to go near him (30:10), and devised every means possible to humiliate him and aggravate his misery (30:12-15).

Job *must* be justified in the yes of his society. This was what he had begged for. It had seemed to him nothing short of criminal that he should die without vindication (16:18). If he were to die a natural death and be buried, the earth would cover his blood forever, which seemed to him a total denial of justice. True, at the height of his personal quest he had been able to affirm his belief that God would vindicate him, but only "after my skin has been destroyed" (19:26).

That is the most any of us are entitled to expect, vindication before the eternal throne, if our basic motives have been good. We think of innumerable Christian martyrs, who have gone to their deaths in unswerving loyalty to the Lord Jesus Christ. We know that on the day of judgment they will be vindicated in the eyes of their persecutors. Job did not expect vindication on earth, but the Lord graciously conceded it to him. And that is why this passage is so important. It is no fairy-tale ending, but a necessary part of the story.

Job was physically healed, his body cleaned of every defect; he claimed back all his property rights within the community, and prospered in everything he put his hands to. His family, who had so callously spurned him in his suffering, queued up to welcome him back to the community, bringing expensive gifts with them (v.11).

The Lord laid his hand on Job's life and work, and he lived

to old age with enormous prosperity. Above all it is emphasised that his three daughters were stunning beauties, and one can imagine the young bachelors of the town vying with each other to be accepted by Job for their hand in marriage, with all the necessary humbling of their parents as they interceded on behalf of their sons, as was the custom.

"And so he died, old and full of years."

Christian Reflections

Verses 7-11 tell the story of the reconciliation between Job and his community. His three friends, his relatives and neighbours had become his enemies and had hounded him mercilessly for many months, but now he graciously forgives them. They accept his ministrations, and reconciliation is effected between them. His prayer for his enemies is an expression of the grace of God in Job's life. Jesus made the extraordinary demand on his followers that they should love their enemies, pray for them, bless them, and do good to them (Matt. 5:43-48). It certainly demands stunning grace to do so, but can we refuse the demands of Jesus? "Everyone agrees that forgiveness is a good thing, until they have someone to forgive" (C.S. Lewis). Forgiveness must have been an incredible feat for Job to attain in relation to the three friends, and even more so in relation to his community.

The life in harmony with God is a life of ministry to others. How would you apply this rule today in your own relationships? Should the initiative in reconciliation come from you, or from them? Read Matthew 5:23. In this Jesus is our perfect example in his cry from the cross: "Father, forgive them, for they know not what they are doing." Especially consider the significance of the three action words which are used to describe how love expresses itself – pray, bless, and do good to them.

Verse 8: "My servant Job will prayer for you, and I will accept his prayer and not deal with you according to your folly." Job was to exercise a priestly function. We too as Christians are called upon to exercise a priestly function (I Pet. 2:5; Rev. 5:9-10). We are called upon to offer up our *bodies* to God "as living sacrifices, holy and pleasing to God" (Rom. 12:1); to offer praise and "to do good and to share with others, for with such sacrifices God is pleased" (Heb. 13:15-16). Interestingly Paul uses priestly language of the work of evangelism (Rom. 15:15-16), where the converted Gentiles "might become an offering acceptable to God..."

Do you see yourself as a priest before God? The New Testament never uses priestly language of those who minister to the Christian congregation. Instead it uses it of every Christian. Consider seriously what you can do to ensure that you are acting in a priestly way.

Verse 12: "God blessed the latter part of Job's life more than the first." A Happy Ending certainly! But God does not always give a happy ending – except in heaven. Of Jesus the sufferer it is said: "Who for the joy set before him endured the cross, scorning its shame, and sat down at the right hand of the throne of God" (Heb. 12:2). Jesus died in dishonour and shame, but his eyes pierced beyond the grave to the future glory of heaven. The same writer says of Moses: "By faith Moses...chose to be ill-treated.... He regarded disgrace for the sake of Christ as of greater value than the treasures of Egypt, *because he was looking ahead to his reward* " (11:25-26).

It is of the essence of the true Christian life to live by faith, not by sight. Sight demands immediate sensations of health, good fortune, instant provision of needs, protection, etc., etc. Faith hangs on in there even when all these things are absent (2 Cor. 5:6-10).

Box 28 – Job must never know.

When we started out on the adventure of Job, we were fully confident that in the end everything would be explained to him – the WHY? of his suffering. Neither he nor his friends knew anything about Satan's plan to destroy him. Surely now all things would be revealed.

Yet they are not. Satan is never mentioned, and not a word is said by way of explanation as to why Job had suffered so cruelly. For Job himself, it seems, no explanation was necessary. He had met with the Lord, the Lord had justified him in the eyes of his friends and neighbours, and for him this was sufficient. And Job must never know, not in this life anyway. He must still walk the path of faith, trusting that the Lord had done all things for his good. Indeed, Job does not ask for explanation, only for vindication, and this the Lord gave him in abundance.

Job had learnt that Shaddai, the God of his sufferings (see box 6), was the same as Yahweh, the God of grace. The God of grace had, in reality, never abandoned Job, though he had appeared with a different face! Now Job's life had been saturated by grace.

Job: Our Epilogue

I read somewhere that suffering "becomes the pivot upon which we can grow in faith or sink in cynicism", and this is a suitable conclusion to the book of Job. He became angry with God, but he never became cynical, never ceased to cling to the conviction that somehow, somewhere, he would understand.

Len and Velma

They were a couple who attended our church in the latter years of their lives. Both of them died early, in their 50s, and both went through very terrible sufferings. They had both been thoroughly this worldly, and had given little thought to spiritual matters.

Velma spent much of her life suffering from the most terrible rheumatoid arthritis, all over her body. By the time she died she had replacement hips and replacement knees – both, fused ankles so that she walked like a penguin, and a fused neck. Amazingly, she had spent most of her adult life suffering the most incredible pain.

She divorced her husband, from whom she had a son, whom she did not see for eighteen years. She later moved in with Len and they lived together for twenty-five years, man and wife in all but legal terms. Yet suffering had not left her unscarred. A fighter, strong-willed by temperament, her physical restrictions meant that she was continually frustrated, and she became an embittered lady.

She met with a Christian occupational therapist who had herself suffered from a debilitating health problem for a number of years, and who had recently been healed by prayer. Velma's question was, "Will he heal me?" He never did, but she found peace with God and life changed. That is where I knew her. She had developed a most moving habit of referring humorously to her ailments. She called herself a "bionic woman".

Len was a perfect mirror of an earthy man. He had been a fighter pilot during World War II, and their home was decorated with pictures of fighter planes. He was a heavy smoker with a foul tongue. When it came to anything spiritual he would turn arrogant and cynical. Velma's new-found faith made him even more cynical and indifferent, but he did notice a considerable change in her.

One Boxing Day he had a massive aneurysm which caused his aorta to burst. Within a couple of days his two legs were amputated, one above the knee, the other just below the hip. It was cruel to behold this man of physical mastery reduced to a wheel-chair and hardly able even to sit properly. His first reaction was very bitter, as, one feels, he, like Job, had reason to be. He spent the next eighteen months in a life of great discomfort and pain. But he began to accompany Velma to church.

His last three weeks were spent in hospital. I visited him several times. He had mellowed so much, and it was actually a joy to open the Bible and read to him, and pray for him. One day I read to him from Psalm 23, and those words, "even though I walk through the valley of the shadow of death, I will fear no evil, for you are with me." I felt a little uncomfortable reading these words to him, but they hit the mark, and he told me on the next visit that after my reading he had gone in his wheelchair to the hospital chapel. As no one was there, he wheeled his chair to the front and prayed in a strong, clear voice, thanking God for his life and offering it back for whatever might be facing him. As he turned to go, a lady was sitting at the back in tears. She said that she had been amazed to hear a person in his condition thanking God. Len had most certainly turned from cynicism to faith.

I would like to think that all suffering Christians won through to a positive, creative reaction to pain, but it has not been so in my experience. I have sadly watched some people go under in an anger which terminated in cynicism, which in turn has led to a crippled emotional and social life.

What lessons do we learn from Job?
First, there is the danger of glorification of suffering. When chloroform was first introduced, there were Christians who opposed it, on the grounds that pain was an essential part of suffering, and good for the soul! Job would have strongly disagreed. And it must be said emphatically that there is no cause and effect relationship between suffering and growth in grace.

Let it be said emphatically that there is no learning value in suffering in itself. What counts is the way we react in the face of suffering. We may say that necessity is the mother of invention, but necessity is not, therefore, good. Suffering is never beneficial in itself and must be fought against, with a positive, active, creative suffering. We must either reform it creatively, or go under.

What is more, one should not reach acceptance except through rebellious anger. The sufferer's Why? should not be discouraged, or made to feel guilty, or repressed. We must enable the victim "to make good use of his sufferings" (Pascal). We must say NO to the suffering, but we win through to the YES. No and Yes must always be there in healthy tension. The YES is not a shallow capitulation, but a hard-won victory over the NO.

Resign yourself? No! A docile, morose, unfruitful attitude – a failure. That which disturbs our lives, puts us out, irritates us, annoys us, makes us suffer – does not of itself make us grow and develop, but it does provide the conditions in which growth and development become possible. Every deprivation, every suffering, can be the occasion for a new surge of creative response. (The thoughts in these paragraphs have been adapted from *Creative Suffering* by Swiss psychologist, Paul Tournier, which I read years ago. Just three days ago I stumbled across the notes I had taken down, in my 1987 diary.)

Jesus in Gethsemane is the supreme example of creative suffering. He did not face the suffering of the Cross with composure, tranquillity, acceptance, but with deep distress: "He began to be deeply distressed and troubled. My soul is overwhelmed with sorrow to the point of death" (Mark 14:34). He pleaded with his Father: "Take this cup from me. Yet not what I will, but what you will." This sacrifice of Jesus, this self-humiliation, this wrestling to understand the purposes of God, is the heart of our understanding of suffering.